LIVING WITH HOUSEPLANTS

Green Foliage Plants

TORSTAR BOOKS
NEW YORK · TORONTO

Torstar Books Inc, 41 Madison Avenue, Suite 2900, New York, NY 10010 in collaboration with ICA-förlaget AB, Västerås, Sweden.

© Torstar Books Inc, 1986, except for photographs pp. 1 and 4–63 © ICA-förlaget 1981, 1985

All rights reserved.
No part of this book may be reproduced in any form or by any means, either electronic or mechanical, including photocopying, recording, or by any information storage and retrieval system, without permission in writing from the publisher.

Library of Congress Cataloging-in-Publication Data
Green foliage plants.
  (Living with houseplants)
  Includes index.
  1. House plants. 2. Foliage plants.
I. Torstar Books (Firm) II. Series.
SB419.G698 1986   635.9′65   86–11308

ISBN 1–55001–064–6 (Living With Houseplants Series)
ISBN 1–55001–058–1 (Green Foliage Plants)

10 9 8 7 6 5 4 3 2 1
Printed in Belgium

CONTENTS

Umbrella plant (*Cyperus alternifolius*)	4
Ornamental figs	6
Trailing and climbing figs	12
Trevesia (*Trevesia palmata*)	14
Common myrtle (*Myrtus communis*)	16
Introducing ferns	18
Maidenhair fern (*Adiantum*)	19
Sword fern (*Nephrolepis exaltata*)	20
Mother fern (*Asplenium bulbiferum*)	22
Bird's nest fern (*Asplenium nidus*)	23
Squirrel's foot fern (*Davallia trichomanoides*)	24
Staghorn fern (*Platycerium bifurcatum*)	25
Cretan brake (*Pteris cretica*)	26
Cloak fern (*Didymochlaena truncatula*)	27
Philodendron (*Philodendron*)	28
Norfolk Island pine (*Araucaria heterophylla*)	32
"Miniature bamboo" (*Pogonatherum paniceum*)	34
Eucalyptus (*Eucalyptus*)	36
Introducing palms	38
Parlor palm (*Chamaedorea elegans*)	39
Yellow palm (*Chrysalidocarpus lutescens*)	40
Fishtail palm (*Caryota*)	41
Coconut palm (*Cocos nucifera*)	42
Date palm (*Phoenix dactylifera*)	44
Desert fan palm (*Washingtonia filifera*)	46
Screw pine (*Pandanus veitchii*)	47
Sago plant (*Cycas revoluta*)	48
House holly (*Cyrtomium falcatum*)	49
Swiss cheese plant (*Monstera deliciosa*)	50
Elephant-foot plant (*Beaucarnea recurvata*)	52
Cardamom (*Elettaria cardamomum*)	54
Stenochlaena (*Stenochlaena tenuifolia*)	56
Schefflera (*Schefflera arboricola, Schefflera actinophylla*)	57
Jacaranda (*Jacaranda mimosifolia*)	60
Yucca (*Yucca elephantipes*)	62
Plants for cool rooms	64
Plants for temperate rooms	66
Plants for warm rooms	68
"Do-it-yourself" plants	69
Index	70
Acknowledgments	72

Umbrella plant
CYPERUS ALTERNIFOLIUS

The umbrella plant is an interesting choice to open this guide to green foliage houseplants because it combines a "primitive" appeal with a strikingly modern elegance. Closely related species include the Egyptian paper-rush (*Cyperus papyrus*), used in ancient times for the making of paper.

The umbrella plant comes from Madagascar (an island off the east coast of Africa), where it thrives in wet, marshy conditions. This means that it is a houseplant that will not object to overwatering (a common cause of death in other plants). On the other hand it will demand constant moisture. One way to make sure that the plant is not deprived of the water it needs is to keep the pot standing permanently in a shallow, water-filled saucer or pan. Another is to grow it hydroponically, as illustrated below.

In the wild, the umbrella plant will reach a height of about 4 feet. Grown indoors in a pot, it is likely to reach 3 feet or perhaps a little more. About twelve narrow, grasslike bracts are produced at the end of long, straight stems. It is the resemblance of these bracts to the spokes of an umbrella that earned the plant its common name. In the summer, small pale brown or greenish flowers appear from the base of the bracts.

The dwarf umbrella plant (*Cyperus alternifolius* 'Gracilis'), which comes from Australia, is unlikely to grow taller than 18 inches.

The ideal way to propagate the umbrella plant is by dividing the roots. This is a fairly simple procedure that can be carried out at any time. Simply remove the plant from its pot and, with a sharp knife, cut down through the root ball to a sufficient depth to allow your fingers and thumbs to disentangle the mass of roots (see also p. 34).

An alternative method of propagation is to cut off the top inch or so of a stem, at the same time reducing the leafy bracts by about half their length. Set each stem in a glass of water or in damp sand or vermiculite. Roots will soon develop and the cuttings can then be transferred to a pot. Cuttings should be kept in bright light and at a temperature of 70°F.

The best time for repotting umbrella plants is the early spring. If plants have not outgrown their pots, then this would also be a good time to top dress with a good commercial potting mix.

Brown tips on the leafy bracts may mean that the air surrounding the plant is too dry.

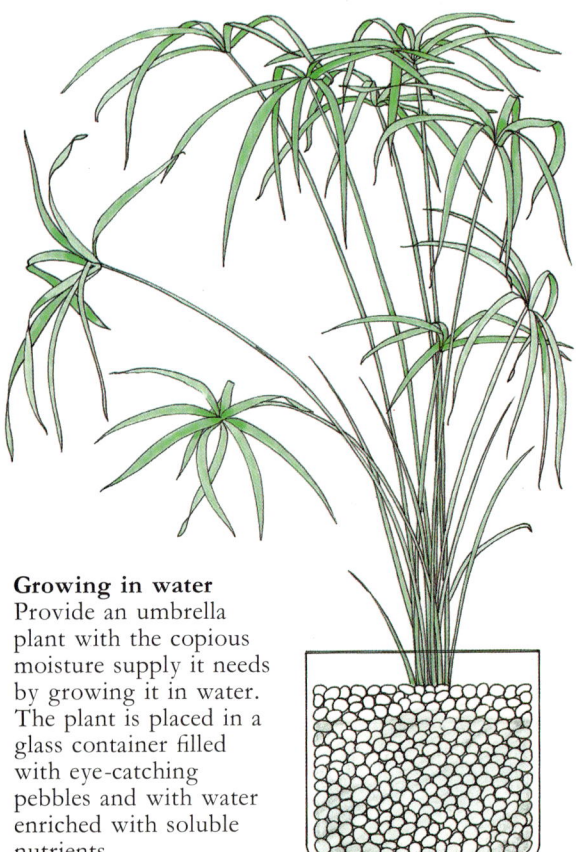

Growing in water
Provide an umbrella plant with the copious moisture supply it needs by growing it in water. The plant is placed in a glass container filled with eye-catching pebbles and with water enriched with soluble nutrients.

GREEN THUMB GUIDE

Watering and feeding
The umbrella plant needs constant moisture, but make sure that the stems are not below the soil surface, since such exposure will eventually cause them to rot. Be extra-attentive in the summer months, when moisture loss will be greatest due to evaporation and spray the foliage regularly. Apply the same treatment to plants kept in dry, centrally-heated atmospheres.

Feed once every two weeks from March through September.

Light and temperature
When grown indoors umbrella plants need good light – about four hours of direct sunlight, when possible, in winter. They will tolerate temperatures between 50°F and 70°F.

Soil
Use a soil mix with a high organic matter content. Add pieces of charcoal to the soil to keep it fresh.

The slender leafy bracts of the umbrella plant contrast well with crisply painted woodwork. A window sill is an ideal situation for this plant.

Ornamental figs

Plants ranging from towering trees to low-growing creepers belong to the ornamental fig, or *Ficus*, family (Moraceae). About 2,000 species grow wild in tropical and subtropical areas, including the mulberry, edible figs and the rubber tree grown for commercial purposes, *Hevea brasiliensis*. All have the milky sap, or latex, for which rubber trees are famed.

Many species of the family are grown as houseplants. The stately rubber plant – a different species from the commercial tree – has adorned living rooms since Victorian times and continues to be popular.

Almost all ficuses are sturdy plants but some problems can occur. The most common are the shedding of leaves, or leaves turning brown at the edges. This most often happens when you first purchase your plant, take it from the steamy conditions of the garden center or greenhouse and place it in a dry indoor atmosphere. Spray the plant copiously during its first few weeks in your home to keep humidity high, and continue to spray occasionally during the summer months. Avoid exposing your plant to sudden cold drafts and too high temperatures – particularly after any change in environment. Never let the soil dry out completely, and water carefully with tepid water.

The creeping fig (*F. pumila*) is a fast-growing trailing plant, ideal for a hanging basket. It also looks attractive placed on a shelf so that its luxuriant foliage cascades downward. This fig is one of the most delicate of its family and will die if neglected and left without water. Its aerial roots can be trained to cling to a moss totem pole, eventually making a pleasing display.

A pretty variety of creeping fig, *F. pumila* 'Variegata', has small, white or cream-colored spots on its leaves. This is a more demanding plant than its relative, needing slightly better light and more warmth.

The familiar rubber plant (*F. elastica*), so loved by the Victorians, can grow to a height of 6 or 7 feet. It is a handsome plant, despite its rather formal appearance. Prune it in the spring to keep its shape good and its size under control.

Currently one of the most popular ficuses, the weeping fig (*F. benjamina*) is a more graceful, treelike plant, with pretty bark like that of a silver birch. It grows to a height of 2 to 18 feet, but will tolerate harsh cutting back. Do not give the plant too much water after pruning or shaping.

Ficus plants can be propagated by two methods: tip cuttings and air layering. The tip cutting method can only be used for the trailing figs, *F. pumila* and *F. radicans*. Cut 2 to 4 inches off the leading growth stem or off a side branch,

The Banyan tree (*Ficus benghalensis*) of India and Sri Lanka can grow to enormous dimensions, with huge aerial roots that grow downward from its branches and act as props to support the heavy crown. One specimen can shelter 1000 people beneath its vast canopy of foliage.

GREEN THUMB GUIDE

Watering and feeding
Do not overwater a ficus. Overwatering causes leaves to fall and roots to rot. The amount of water needed varies between tree types and creeping types of fig. In the growing season, creeping figs need to be kept moist. For tree types, however, allow the soil to dry out partially before watering. In winter it is important to use tepid water for all kinds of fig.

Ficus plants, particularly creeping types, will appreciate being misted occasionally with water. Sponge the leaves regularly to keep them shiny and free of clogging dust. Feed with good standard fertilizer every two weeks from May through September, and occasionally during the rest of the year.

Light and temperature
Tree types of ficus thrive in a bright well-lit position, but not in direct sunlight. Creeping figs do better in partial shade. Always avoid placing a fig in drafts or too near excessive heat – central heating radiators for example. Ideally the temperature should not exceed 70°F, nor fall below 50°F.

Soil
Any ordinary potting soil containing peat moss is fine for both types of fig. Repot in spring but not more than every two years.

immediately below a node (the point where a leaf is attached to the stem). Place the cutting in a glass of water, removing the leaves below the water.

Once some roots have appeared, transfer the cutting to a 3-inch pot containing a moistened mixture of equal parts of peat moss and sand or perlite. When the new plant has become established, usually about four months later, move it to a pot one size larger containing standard potting mix.

To propagate by air layering, make a shallow cut into the plant's stem all the way around and cover the wounded part with moist sphagnum moss. Wrap the moss in a piece of plastic and tie securely at both ends with string or a twist tie. Keep the moss constantly damp.

Two months later, new roots will start to appear through the moss. Sever the stem with the clump of moss and roots from the parent plant, pot it up and treat it as a new plant.

The rubber plant (*Ficus elastica* 'Robusta') has shiny, dark-green leaves on a single stem and can grow to a height of 10 feet or more. Combined with other plants to soften its formal shape, it is most impressive.

The Moreton bay fig (*Ficus macrophylla*) is best grown as a shrub. Shape it by regularly cutting back the branch tips.

A variety of rubber plant, *F. elastica* 'Schrijveriana' has pretty cream-edged leaves, mottled with cream and dark green. It needs a warmer position and better light than the green plants.

Known as the fiddle-leaf fig because its gleaming leaves are shaped rather like the body of a violin, *Ficus lyrata* comes from the forests of West Africa. When grown indoors, it reaches a height of 7 feet, with leaves 15 inches long by 9 inches wide. This decorative foliage is dark green, with lighter undersides and prominent midribs and veins.

Ficus wildemaniana (sometimes mistakenly labeled *F. pandurata*) is a sturdy plant from West Africa. On a mature specimen, the shapely leaves can be almost 10 inches long. An adaptable fig, it tolerates low light conditions, and is useful as part of a display with other plants.

Ficus benghalensis 'Krishnae' is similar to the bengal fig, below, but has gray-green, slightly funnel-shaped leaves. These leaves are downy and hairy and must be sprayed with water regularly to keep them clean. In summer, stand the plant outside to be washed by rain.

Ficus rubiginosa (syn. *F. australis*) is an Australian plant, known as the rusty fig because of the rust-colored powder which dusts the underside of its leaves. Indoors, it grows to a height of 3 to 4 feet, with dark-green leaves 3 to 6 inches long. A similar but variegated plant, *F. rubiginosa* 'Variegata' has attractive cream, gray and green marbled leaves.

The bengal fig (*Ficus benghalensis*), when grown indoors, will not attain the proportions of its counterpart in the wild. The indoor variety grows only to 6 feet high and has dark-green, oval-shaped leaves up to 1 foot long covered with fine reddish-brown hairs.

The weeping fig (*Ficus benjamina*) has become one of the most popular, small-leafed ficus plants. In its tropical Indian, Asian and Australian home it grows to 40 feet, but as a houseplant it averages only 6 feet. Its shiny green leaves are 2 to 4 inches long and droop gracefully from their stalks like willow leaves.

Ficus leprieurii (*syn. F. triangularis*) has unusual leaves that are almost triangular in shape. Like all shiny leaves, these should be sponged regularly with a damp cloth to keep them free of dust. Dust both spoils their appearance and interferes with photosynthesis.

The mistletoe fig, *Ficus deltoidea* (*syn. F. diversifolia*) is an attractive miniature tree from west Malaysia. Well worth growing for its gray-green, triangular leaves, flecked with translucent silver, it also bears masses of small inedible berries. These cluster at the leaf axils and are bright green when they first appear, turning red or yellow in sunshine. Display the plant by a window facing east or west, but note that it will also tolerate direct sun in a south-facing window. If the plant is in full sunshine, keep it well watered or its leaves will discolor and fall off.

A native of the forests of Zaire in Africa, *Ficus buxifolia* has only recently been grown as a houseplant. Its small green leaves, similar to those of *F. Benjamina*, are shiny, roughly triangular in shape and measure about an inch across. They are attached at intervals along reddish branches that bend and arch slightly, giving the plant a graceful shape. Indoors, this plant usually grows to 3 or 4 feet high, very occasionally to as much as 6 feet. *F. buxifolia* is an adaptable, easy-to-grow plant that makes an attractive feature in any well lit room.

The Indian laurel (*Ficus microcarpa*, commonly misnamed *F. retusa*) is a native of southeast Asia and Australia. It can be grown in hedges and is a popular plant in Israel and Egypt for bordering grand avenues. Whether grown as a shrub or tree, it has aerial roots and shiny, usually pointed, leaves which grow to about 3 inches long. A more upright plant than *F. benjamina* which it resembles, the Indian laurel bears many branching stems. As it matures, shoots can be taken out to train the plant into shape. It will occasionally produce inedible fruit.

Trailing and climbing figs

The creeping or Chinese fig, *Ficus pumila*, actually comes from Japan, North Vietnam and Australia as well as the warmer parts of China. In the wild it uses its ivylike roots to attach itself to trees or rock faces.

As an indoor plant the stems, bearing thin, heart-shaped leaves, may reach over 2 feet in length. The creeping fig will tolerate a temperature range between 50°F and 70°F. It dislikes direct sunlight, preferring north- east- or west-facing windows. It is a fast-growing trailer ideal for hanging baskets.

Another attractive way to show off the Chinese fig is to allow it to climb up or around a shaped support. The wreath shapes shown here would probably be available from most garden centers, along with numerous other shapes ranging from animals to candelabras. To make your own, create the basic shape from plastic-covered wire, insert this framework in the container and then wrap a layer of sphagnum moss around it, securing it with wire.

Cleaning leaves
1 Wipe shiny-leaved species with a leaf polish as shown.
2 Spray dull or hairy leaves with water.

Ficus sagittata (*syn. F. radicans*) is an equally adaptable fig. It makes an impressive climber but will also do well in a hanging basket. The beautiful white-and-green leaf shown above is from the wiry-stemmed *F. radicans* 'Variegata.'

Trevesia
TREVESIA PALMATA

This native of tropical Asia, Malaya and the Pacific islands has highly decorative leaves with an uncanny resemblance to the webbed footprints of a goose. A similar variety, *Trevesia palmata* 'Micholitzii' has leaves up to 2 feet across, which have a delicate lacy look like enormous snowflakes. A member of the Araliaceae family, *Trevesia palmata* was named in honor of the family of Treves de Bonfigli of Padua in Italy, who were supporters of botanical research.

In its natural habitat, *T. palmata* grows to 20 feet high and bears greenish-white flowers, each measuring about an inch across. Its shoots are covered with reddish hair, but its leaves, which can be as much as 2 feet long, are practically smooth. The cultivated plant looks a little like the Japanese aralia (*Fatsia japonica*), but each lobe of the leaves is more deeply cut. *T. palmata* is also taller than the Japanese aralia: in two or three years, plants reach a height of 4 to 5 feet with leaves up to 18 inches wide. Unfortunately, it does not flower indoors.

As a houseplant, *T. palmata* needs plenty of space, since it grows so quickly. To look its best, it demands to be the focal point of a room, perhaps with a plain-colored background, such as a pale wall, to contrast with the dramatic outlines of its foliage. Displayed effectively, it will grace any living area or office suite and amply reward the attention lavished on it.

A pretty, patterned container can enhance its greenery. Remember always to choose a pot smaller than the plant itself, or you will have a pot full of wet soil that will damage the plant's roots and possibly even kill it.

T. palmata is a fairly robust plant but can be affected by red spider mites, which make its leaves curl and stunt its growth. Destroy mites with a systemic pesticide at the first sign of trouble.

Propagate *T. palmata* from seed or by stem cuttings. If you can obtain seeds, sow them to a depth of one inch in a heated propagating case filled with moistened rooting mix. Keep the temperature of the case at between 60°F and 65°F and place it in bright, filtered light.

When the seedlings have grown several inches high, transfer them to small pots containing standard potting mix. Given sufficient care they should quickly grow into sturdy new plants.

Propagation by stem cuttings is a more challenging process. Take cuttings 2 to 3 inches long from the base of the plant. Dip the ends in hormone rooting powder and plant the cuttings in 3-inch pots, filled with a moistened mixture of peat moss and coarse sand or perlite in equal quantities. Envelop the pot in a plastic bag to create a mini-greenhouse, and keep in bright, filtered light at a temperature of about 60°F.

Four to six weeks later, the cuttings should have rooted. Remove the plastic bag and add enough water to keep the soil barely moist. Apply a liquid fertilizer every two weeks. Three to six months after the start of propagation the cuttings should be mature enough to move to slightly larger pots.

GREEN THUMB GUIDE

Watering and feeding
In summer, water this fast-growing plant generously, keeping the potting mix thoroughly moist. In the winter rest period, water more sparingly and allow the top half inch of soil to dry out between waterings. Feed with liquid fertilizer every two weeks during the active growing period.

Light and temperature
T. palmata *thrives in bright light and a position by an east- or west-facing window is ideal. If placed in poor light, it will become thin and pale. The warmth of an average living room suits it well, but the temperature should not exceed 70°F. In winter, do not let the temperature drop below 50°F.*

Soil
Use a standard potting mix, with a quarter part of coarse sand or perlite. Because it grows so fast, T. palmata *should be repotted every spring into a pot one size larger. Once the maximum pot size has been reached, simply top dress the soil.*

Trevesia palmata makes an impressive and luxuriant display in any situation.

Common myrtle
MYRTUS COMMUNIS

Highly aromatic foliage, attractive flowers and, often, decorative fruits are all features shared by plants in the myrtle family. The common myrtle is a native of the Mediterranean region and the Middle East where it grows to a height of about 17 feet. In other warm, dry climates the myrtle grows as a shrub, rather than a tree, and is often used in gardens where it is clipped and pruned to grow in bushes or hedges.

As an indoor plant this bushy evergreen will grow to a height of 2 to 3 feet. Its small, tapered oval leaves give off a fragrant aroma when rubbed between the fingers. Between summer and mid fall it will produce small white flowers, about an inch wide, each with a central cluster of delicate yellow stamens. These are followed by blue-black berries.

For any indoor gardener interested in practicing the art of topiary, the common myrtle would be a good plant to start on. In order to produce a dense and sturdy base on which to begin experimenting, keep on pinching out the growing tips at regular intervals. The plant can be pruned at any time of year, to give an attractive ornamental shape. But do not be too enthusiastic. Overpruning will mean that the plant produces fewer flowers or none at all. Once you have achieved the shape you want, keep it by pruning only the strong growing shoots which would otherwise destroy its outline. Older plants that have become bare around the base of the stem can be cut back severely.

Because it has a woody stem, myrtle is an ideal subject for propagation by heel cuttings (see below). Alternatively, during the spring, top cuttings can be taken from stems or shoots that have recently matured. Root them in a sandy mix, covering the container with a plastic bag to make sure the soil does not dry out.

Do not allow a myrtle plant to become too dry, since it will then be susceptible to attack by red spider mites. These sap-sucking pests feed from the underside of the leaves which then become speckled with yellow blotches and fall prematurely. To get rid of red spider mite, cut away infested leaves then use a systemic insecticide.

GREEN THUMB GUIDE

Watering and feeding
Water regularly from spring through fall, but sparingly in the winter rest period. Do not allow the plant to become too dry, since this will cause the leaves to fall. Dryness in myrtle also makes it vulnerable to red spider mite. Ideally, use rain water or lime-free water.

Myrtle needs only a little feeding. From March through July it should be fed every second week with a liquid fertilizer. Mist the leaves frequently to help prevent leaf fall.

Light and temperature
During the winter rest period, the myrtle does best in a light, well-ventilated rather cool room at a temperature that does not drop below 40°F. Turn the plant regularly if you want it to grow symmetrically.

Excessive warmth (between 68°F and 72°F) will cause the plant to shed its leaves and prevent flowering. During the summer months it can stand outside on a balcony, sundeck or porch, but keep it in the shade.

Soil and repotting
If necessary, repot every spring, using a humus-rich standard soil mixed with one third coarse sand or perlite. Avoid repotting old plants.

Heel cuttings
Propagate myrtle by cutting off side shoots, taking at the same time a "heel" or small piece of the main stem. Trim the heel to the shape shown. Fill a pot with rooting mixture, make holes with a pencil and insert the cuttings, which may be dipped in hormone rooting powder before planting.

Myrtles will produce a profusion of star-shaped white blooms if the plant has been kept cool in winter. The fragrant flowers are each about ¾ inch cross.

The common myrtle lends itself to imaginative pruning to produce ornamental shapes. Its glossy leaves release a fragrant aroma when crushed.

Introducing ferns

Homemakers of the nineteenth century, taking their cues from Victorian England, were passionately fond of ferns and grew large collections of them in conservatories or in specially-constructed Wardian or glass cases. Today, ferns are making a comeback, although they no longer need special growing conditions. With the advent of central heating, the toxic fumes from coal fires are no longer a problem.

Mysterious and even magical properties were, for centuries, attributed to ferns. The reason was that the way they reproduced themselves remained an enigma until the mid-nineteenth century. Now it is well known that the spores (usually found on fertile spore-bearing fronds) play a crucial role in the process of fern reproduction.

In nature, the reproductive process of a fern is set in motion when the spores fall to the ground and begin to absorb moisture. In order to encourage the process at home you could try standing a pot of ferns inside another container filled with moist potting mix. This, however, is a somewhat random method. To be really sure of obtaining new plants, either propagate by division, or by layering bulbils (plantlets carried on the fronds of ferns such as the mother fern, *Asplenium bulbiferum*). The deliberate cultivation of spores is also possible.

Most of the ferns that are grown indoors also grow wild in the subtropical and tropical regions of the world. Some are found on the forest floor while others, such as the bird's nest fern (*Asplenium nidus*) and the squirrel's foot fern, on the trunks and branches or in the forks of trees. The more closely you can match the conditions in which ferns thrive in the wild, the more successful you are likely to be in keeping them healthy in your home.

Whether they come from temperate or tropical zones, all ferns love moisture. Add to this dappled, filtered light and, most important, fresh air (or as close to fresh as is possible), and you should be successful. Aim for a temperature of between 60°F and 70°F and position plants out of direct sunlight. Grouping plants will help keep the humidity level high, and will also look attractive.

Ferns are tremendously versatile and they will make a stunning contribution to any setting.

The delta maidenhair fern (*Adiantum radrianum syn. A. cuneatum*) from Brazil is one of the most popular indoor ferns. A charming and delicate-looking plant, it is not difficult to cultivate. It is an ideal plant for a terrarium, but will look equally good in a hanging basket contrasted with a trailing fern. It grows to about $1\frac{1}{2}$ feet and likes high humidity.

Maidenhair fern
ADIANTUM

Adiantums, commonly called maidenhair ferns, are the most popular of all pot-grown ferns. The genus has worldwide distribution, but it is the ferns that grow naturally in warmer regions that are most suitable to cultivate as houseplants. Those from temperate areas are less adaptable, since they do not favor the all-year warmth of most home environments.

There are several varieties of maidenhair ferns, all of which have their own special attraction. The common name comes from the fact that their fine, shiny, often black leafstalks resemble human hair. The fronds of *A. raddianum* (*syn. A. cuneatum*), the delta maidenhair, are often used in floral bouquets.

The plant may grow to a height of 18 inches with a spread of up to 24 inches, and the dark-green, triangular fronds may be 8 inches long and 6 inches at their widest point. They are then divided into numerous D-shaped leaflets or pinnae, hence the name delta maidenhair. There are a number of named forms including 'Decorum', 'Fragrantissimum' which has denser foliage with a pronounced fragrance, and 'Fritz-Luthii' which has dense overlapping pinnae.

A. capillus-veneris, also known as Venushair, like other maidenhair ferns, will contribute an air of delicacy and relaxation to any setting. This particular specimen has light-green fronds that may grow to 24 inches long and 10 inches wide. It is also tolerant of cooler conditions. *A. tenerum* (brittle or fan maidenhair) can grow up to 3 feet in height and has triangular light-green fronds, with many delicate fan-shaped pinnae that are fringed or crested at the edges. Other forms include *A.t.* 'Farleyense' (glory fern) which has drooping fronds with deeply cut frilly-edged pinnae, and *A.t.* 'Wrightii' whose young fronds are pink but when mature turn fresh green. *A. hispidulum* (Australian maidenhair) seldom grows more than 12 inches tall and has hairy stalks and stiff fronds divided into pointed fingerlike sections. Young fronds have a bronze hue.

The fronds of adiantums rise from fast-spreading rhizomes that grow horizontally just below the surface of the potting mix. The best time to propagate is in the spring when the rhizome can be divided. Take the entire plant from its pot and shake the potting mix away from the roots. Then cut the rhizome into as many pieces as required, but make sure that each piece has a few fronds growing from it. Set the rhizome section in a 3-inch pot containing a peat-based mix which will allow water retention at the same time as providing adequate drainage. Do not cover it with soil. It should simply rest on the surface of the mix. The newly potted rhizome should be enclosed in a plastic bag and kept in a warm and shady place until roots form. Rooting will have taken place within a month or so. The covering can then be removed. Water sparingly for the next four weeks, following the same procedure as for established plants. Then treat as mature specimens.

GREEN THUMB GUIDE

Watering and feeding
Maidenhair ferns only need moderate watering, but the roots should be kept moist. Avoid excessive watering, since this will cause the roots to rot. Allow the top inch of the potting mix to dry out between waterings. Apply a standard liquid fertilizer occasionally during the active growth period.

Light and temperature
Provide either medium light or bright filtered light. Direct sunlight must be avoided, since it will scorch the tender fronds, although in the winter occasional early-morning sunlight will encourage continuous growth. To prevent the plant from becoming lopsided, it is advisable to rotate it in the direction of the light every two or three days. These ferns will happily grow in normal room temperatures and will tolerate a minimum of 50°F. It is particularly important not to place them in cold drafts. If the room temperature rises above 75°F, stand the pots on trays of moist pebbles and mist daily to achieve the correct level of humidity.

Soil and repotting
Use a standard potting mix or make one consisting of equal parts of peat moss, leaf mold and coarse sand or perlite. Maintain good drainage at all times. Repot either in the spring or early summer when a surface-creeping rhizome has covered the potting mix and is beginning to spread over the rim of the pot.

Sword fern
NEPHROLEPIS EXALTATA

Although about 2,000 species of fern are actually suitable for growing indoors, only a fraction of them are available commercially. For most people, a typical fern is likely to be a member of the genus *Nephrolepis*, and more particularly the sword fern or the Boston fern.

The sword fern (*Nephrolepis exaltata*) is the commonest and probably the most popular of all ferns grown as houseplants. Much larger and coarser than the erect sword fern (*Nephrolepis cordifolia*), its deeply slashed pale-green fronds can reach a length of 4 to 6 feet. In the erect variety the fronds grow to only about 2 feet and are much narrower.

The Boston fern (*Nephrolepis exaltata Bostoniensis*), with its broad, fast-growing feathery fronds, is another great favorite in modern living rooms. The Royal Botanical Gardens at Kew in England named it the Boston fern in honor of the grower in Boston, Massachusetts, who first brought this mutation of *N. exaltata* to prominence.

Other easily obtainable varieties of *N. exaltata* include the lace fern, *N.e.* 'Whitmanii' and *N.e.* 'Rooseveltii' both of which have finely divided feathery fronds growing up to 3 feet long.

All the different varieties have fronds which rise from an upright "underground" rhizome, the top of which looks like a short, thick stem. From this rhizome grow slender furry runners which put down roots at intervals, from which small new plantlets arise. These can be potted as new plants.

Select a rooted runner and, using a sharp knife, cut it about 2 inches from the tip. This section can then be planted in a 3-inch pot of standard peat-based potting mix. Treat the new plant as a mature specimen.

It is also possible to propagate nephrolepis spores, and details of the various stages involved in spore propagation are given on page 27.

While a cascading mass of pale-green fronds is an attractive and impressive feature in any room, do not be beguiled by interior design magazines showing ferns flourishing in lightless bathrooms or dimly lit hallways. They will put up with shade, certainly, but in too dark a spot they will soon start to lose their fronds.

Remember, also, that hanging baskets, particularly in centrally-heated rooms, dry out very quickly. To make watering less of a chore, hang the basket at eye level, or, if it must be higher, fix it with a pulley. To avoid drips on the carpets or furniture, buy a basket that is fitted with a drip tray. You will find instructions on how to prepare a hanging basket on the opposite page. It is important to make sure that it is fixed securely, for once filled with a plant, soil and water it will be very heavy.

Nephrolepis exaltata 'Rooseveltii' has feathery dark-green fronds that may grow to 3 feet.

The fronds of *Nephrolepis cordifolia*, taper from about 4 inches at the base to $\frac{1}{4}$ inch at the tip.

Indoor ferns are usually associated with *Nephrolepis exaltata*, the sword fern. With deeply slashed fronds falling in graceful arches, a mature specimen will enhance any setting.

MAKING A HANGING BASKET

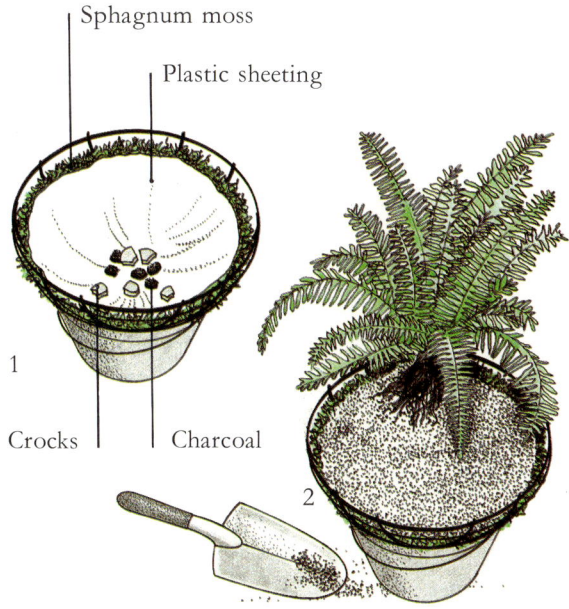

GREEN THUMB GUIDE

Watering and feeding
Never let the compost dry out, but do not overwater, for this will lead to rotten roots. As long as the room temperature remains above 50°F, plants should be watered as often as necessary to keep the soil thoroughly moist. If the temperature falls below 55°F for more than two days, let the top third of the mixture dry out between waterings. Feed with a standard liquid fertilizer once every two weeks between March and August. Over 70°F, increase humidity.

Light and temperature
Position plants in bright light, but not direct sunlight. Sword ferns will tolerate medium shade for up to five weeks.

Soil
Use a standard peat-based potting mix with a quarter of sharp sand or ground vermiculite. Or use half soil-based mix with half leaf mold.

Ferns of many kinds are ideal subjects for a hanging basket. Make such a basket as follows:
1 Line a wire basket with sphagnum moss and then with a layer of plastic sheeting. Place a few crocks and pieces of charcoal inside for drainage and keeping the soil sweet smelling.
2 Fill the basket with potting mix, then plant with ferns and other plants, as desired. Water well, then leave in a moderately lit place for a few days to allow the plants to settle down. Suspend the basket from a ceiling hook with strong decorative chains or ropes.

Mother fern
ASPLENIUM BULBIFERUM

The graceful fronds of the mother fern have central black stems and finely cut, medium-green leaves. Provided it has warm, moist, shady conditions, the fern is quite hardy and easy to care for.

These three young plants, or bulbils, have been pinched off the mother fern's frond and can now be potted in moist peaty soil. Within four weeks they should show new growth and can be transferred to new pots. These bulbils provide a constant supply of new mother ferns to add to your collection. Alternatively, they would make attractive gifts for friends.

A member of the spleenwort family of ferns, the mother fern (*Asplenium bulbiferum*) is a graceful plant, which looks pretty in a hanging basket. It is a native of Australia and New Zealand, and as a houseplant grows up to 4 feet tall, with a spread of 2 to 3 feet. Each frond is 8 or 9 inches wide, with 20 or 30 leaves (pinnae) branching off its main black stem.

With their finely cut leaves, the delicate lacy fronds of this fern are a little like parsley or even carrot leaves – one common name of the fern is parsley fern. Mother fern, however, is its most popular name, given for its habit of bearing young plants, or bulbils, on the upper side of mature fronds.

In spring each of these bulbils can be gently pinched off when it has three or four fronds of its own, and potted in moist peaty soil. Several bulbils can be placed in one pot. Water sparingly, just enough to moisten the soil, then enclose the whole pot in a plastic bag to keep the humidity high. Keep the pot in a slightly shaded position at normal room temperature.

After about four weeks the plants will show more top growth. Reduce humidity gradually by removing the bag for longer periods each day. Water only enough to keep the soil moist and do not feed at this stage. Once growth is well underway, repot each plant and treat it as an adult. In nature, the budding bulbils grow until they weigh the parent frond down to the ground. The young plants then take root in the soil in their mother's shade.

Mother ferns prefer moist, shady conditions in a temperature above 50°F but not much higher than 75°F. Like all ferns they like their leaves spray misted regularly to keep humidity high. Any brown flecks on the fronds are a warning that the plant is in too much sun and needs moving to a shadier spot. In their natural habitat, these ferns grow on the sun-dappled floor of the forest, in the shadow of larger plants and trees.

Bird's nest fern
ASPLENIUM NIDUS

Although the bird's nest fern belongs to the same family as the mother fern, it is quite different in appearance. Broad, strap-shaped, apple-green fronds rise from a central brown core in a cluster to form a rosette. Each frond has a dark-brown midrib, bold at the base and fading toward the tip. The edges are wavy and the whole surface of the frond has a corrugated look.

The bird's nest fern is a native of tropical Asia and the Pacific islands. It is an epiphyte and grows high on the branched forks of trees, where it looks much like a nest – hence its name. Rain water collects in its spongy, fibrous central core which retains the moisture for the plant's use. Rotting leaves and other debris also gather there and provide nourishment.

Grown as a houseplant, the bird's nest fern needs more sun, higher temperatures and more water than other ferns but is worth the effort for its striking foliage. The warmer and more humid its surroundings, the larger and more impressive the plant becomes. Because it grows high on trees in its natural habitat rather than on the shady forest floor, it tolerates more sun than most ferns, but does not like to be sited in direct sun. Brown spots on the fronds and a general paling of color warn that the plant is having too much sunshine and not enough humidity. Change the fern's position to give it more shade and spray it regularly.

This fern can be propagated from its spores. If you do wish to try, look out for the brown spore "cases" which develop on the backs of the fronds on either side of the midrib. These contain millions of microscopic spores. Details of how to collect and propagate them are given on page 27.

The third asplenium often grown indoors is *A. daucifolium*. Like *A. bulbiferum*, it has feathery, arching fronds. These may grow to 18 inches in length and about 6 inches wide. This fern, too, produces bulbils on mature fronds, which makes propagation very easy (see *A. bulbiferum*, p. 22).

GREEN THUMB GUIDE

Watering and feeding
In spring and summer, water generously to keep the soil moist and spray mist the fronds daily. In winter, water less but often – just enough to keep the soil from drying out. Feed every two weeks from spring through summer with liquid fertilizer. Do not feed in winter.

Light and temperature
Medium or partial shade suits A. bulbiferum *best – by a north- or east-facing window is ideal.* A. nidus *will do well in a sunnier position. The minimum temperature for* A. bulbiferum *is 50°F;* A. nidus *needs a slightly higher temperature with a minimum of 55°F.*

Soil
Use a standard potting mix for either, or, for A. bulbiferum, *use a mixture of equal parts of fibrous peat, loam and sand.* A. nidus *prefers a more peaty mixture, so use two parts of peat to one of sand and loam. Repot in spring when the roots seem to be filling the pot.*

The unusual solid, straplike fronds of the bird's nest fern are extremely striking. This fern needs more sunlight, moisture and warmth than most others but, with care, should last for many years.

Squirrel's foot fern
DAVALLIA TRICHOMANOIDES

The squirrel's foot fern, also known as *D. bullata* or *D. mariesii*, comes from Malaysia where it lives in the tops of trees. It is an epiphyte, that is, a plant which, in its natural habitat, clings to trees, walls, rocks or other plant supports with its above-ground or aerial roots. It obtains nourishment from airborne debris or from decaying organic matter lodged in the crevices of bark, rocks, and so on.

Other ferns in the same genus include *D. canariensis* (deer's foot fern, see p. 66) and *D. fejeensis* (hare's foot – or rabbit's foot – fern). These common names arise from the curious furry rhizomes that will creep across and down the sides of their containers and bear a striking resemblance to the feet of small furry animals.

The reddish-brown rhizomes of the squirrel's foot fern produce 9-inch long gray-green stalks. These stalks carry dark-green fronds that measure about 9 inches long by 6 inches wide. When grown indoors, the plant will reach a height of about 1 foot.

Epiphytes, which commonly thrive in the treetops in tropical forests, are ideal plants for hanging baskets. In the wild they are likely to receive a good soaking from above – but rainwater quickly drains away. This is precisely the kind of watering available in hanging baskets.

A group of well-established davallias would completely cover the outside of a hanging basket, giving a magnificently sumptuous effect. Hang the basket on a swivel hook so it can be rotated to give an even distribution of light.

An interesting and rather unusual way of displaying these ferns is in a fern "ball" which consists of a compact mass of fern roots, such as those of the squirrel's foot fern. Fern balls are usually sold in a dry, dormant state and need to be soaked well before being hung in a warm, moist and shady place.

Propagate in the spring – or when the rhizomes have become too tangled – by cutting 2- to 3-inch sections of rhizome from the parent. Each section should bear one or two fronds. Pin the sections down in a mix of equal parts peat moss, coarse sand and perlite in a 3-inch pot. Do not bury them; let them rest on the surface of the soil. Cover with a plastic bag until rooting takes place (about 3 weeks) then uncover and water as necessary to keep moist.

GREEN THUMB GUIDE

Watering and feeding
The plants should be watered moderately, so that the soil is moist throughout, but do not overwater, since this will lead to rotting. Allow the top half of the potting mix to dry out before watering again. Feed actively growing plants every two weeks.

Light and temperature
The ideal situation for a squirrel's foot fern is in a west- or east-facing window. Direct sunlight will cause the fronds to discolor.

An average room temperature of 70°F is acceptable, although ferns will suffer at more than 75°F or less than 55°F. Centrally-heated homes with relatively dry atmospheres will not affect davallias adversely, although most other ferns prefer a moist atmosphere.

Soil and repotting
Use a potting mix containing soil, peat moss and sand in equal parts.

Give older plants a new lease on life by repotting. Trim off some of the outer roots and detach some of the rhizomes. Then repot plants in fresh mix in their original pots.

The furry mass of rhizomes produced by a well-established squirrel's foot fern can be as attractive as its foliage. Unlike other ferns it does not object to the dry atmosphere of centrally-heated rooms.

Staghorn fern
PLATYCERIUM BIFURCATUM

This curious looking fern grows naturally in the treetops of Australian rain forests. It is not a parasite, using the host tree simply as a place to lodge: it is an epiphyte.

The staghorn belongs to a genus unique among ferns both as far as its form and its lifestyle are concerned, as it possesses two distinctly different types of frond. Most striking are the long, pendulous antlerlike fronds from which the plant gets its name. These are fertile, spore-bearing fronds. They grow from a single, sterile frond which is flatter and shield-shaped.

While it does not produce spores, this frond has other equally important tasks to perform in the wild. Not only does it help anchor the plant to the branch on which it is sited, it is also shaped in such a way that it can catch organic debris, such as leaves, falling from above, and direct it down to the plant's base. Here the debris eventually decomposes, and provides the plant with nutrients.

Staghorn ferns are often sold mounted on slabs of moss-covered wood or bark ready for hanging on walls indoors or outside on trees that do not shed their bark.

Indoor gardeners should also be aware of another important nutritional source for this fern, namely the decaying basal fronds themselves. These fronds are constantly being replaced as tender new bright green fronds unfurl on top of their old, brown and paper dry predecessors. Although they look dead, do not remove them.

Propagate staghorn ferns from the new plants which shoot up from the basal frond. Wait until they are about 3 inches high before cutting below the oldest shield frond of the young plant also taking a small piece of the basal fronds of the parent.

GREEN THUMB GUIDE

Watering and feeding
Water generously in the spring and summer months. The best way to do this, whatever kind of container is being used, is to plunge the roots in water. The basal fronds may cover so much of the soil surface in a pot that it is virtually impossible to water from above. Allow the plant to dry out before the next watering. In the winter, water just enough to keep the potting mix moist.

The staghorn has scant needs for nutrients, but in summer will probably require half a normal dose of liquid fertilizer every two weeks. If the plant is mounted on board or bark, immerse the roots in water to which the fertilizer has been added. Never use chemical fertilizers in granule form. Undissolved granules may cause chemical "burns."

Light and temperature
Provide good, bright light, but not direct sunlight which will cause the fronds to discolor.

Staghorns will tolerate a maximum of 75°F, as long as they are kept moist. Winter temperatures should not drop below 55°F.

Soil and repotting
Soil should be rich in humus and include, if possible, ground or shredded bark. It should also be well aerated, which explains why hanging baskets or mounting barks are preferable to pots. Repotting, if it cannot be avoided, should only be necessary every four to five years.

The dramatic and unusual staghorn fern can also be grown on a strip of bark and mounted on a wall.

Cretan brake
PTERIS CRETICA

The vigorous and easy-to-grow Cretan brake is also known as the ribbon fern, because of the ribbonlike band of spores produced on the undersides of fertile fronds. One of the fern's great attractions is its highly prolific spore production. You are quite likely to be presented with an unexpected bonus of new plants when small pterises begin to emerge from neighboring pots.

One of the most popular pterises, Cretan brake has attractive medium-green fronds up to 12 inches long, growing on 6-inch black stems. The variety *P. cretica* 'Albolineata' is admired for the creamy white bands on either side of the middle ribs of each pinna or frond segment.

In its native Crete, the ribbon fern is found growing wild on limestone walls in shady, damp spots. Indoors, therefore, it will do best in semi-shade and high humidity. If fronds turn brown from lack of moisture, remove them to allow new growth to flourish. When repotting make sure that the root of the fern is only just covered.

Propagate these ferns either from spores or, for quicker results, from rhizome sections. Make sure that each section bears both fronds and roots, then plant it in a 3-inch pot of peat-based mix.

You might consider a grouping of pteris species including the Victoria fern (below left) and the trembling fern (*P. tremula*) whose yellow-green foliage would make a perfect foil to the other two.

GREEN THUMB GUIDE

Watering and feeding
Use tepid, lime-free water to keep the roots moist at all times. But, during cool spells, avoid the risk of waterlogging the potting mix by allowing the top half inch to dry out between waterings. During the growing season, new fronds benefit from a humid atmosphere. So spray often. Feed with a lime-free, salt-free liquid fertilizer, diluted to half-strength, once every two weeks.

Light and temperature
Bright light, but not direct sunlight, is best for Cretan brake. It will thrive in normal room temperatures. But take 55°F as the minimum level of tolerance. Above 65°F you will need to pay special attention to its water requirements. Stand it on moist pebbles to increase humidity and spray with tepid water at regular intervals until the temperature drops.

Soil
Use a peat-based mix or equal parts of peat moss and potting mix. Remember that peat-based mix will need more frequent feeding.

The Victoria fern (*Pteris ensiformis* 'Victoriae') is a dwarf cultivar of *P. ensiformis*. It is much admired for its variegated fronds, with silvery central parts edged with dark-green serrated outlines. Also known as the Queen's fern, it originally came from India.

Cretan brake (*Pteris cretica*) has fronds of medium green that will grow up to 12 inches long on their black stalks.

Cloak fern
DIDYMOCHLAENA TRUNCATULA

The thick, almost leatherlike fronds of the tropical fern *Didymochlaena* (pronounced "diddymoklena") are glossy green and touched with bronze. These features make it a handsome addition to a group of houseplants in a permanently shaded position.

The fronds form in an attractive open rosette on the plant's thick stem, but it is the young ones that bear the bronze tones that make the fern so distinctive. Each frond is some 12 inches in length.

Given shady, moist conditions resembling its natural habitat on the damp tropical forest floor, the plant will adapt with relative ease to the indoor environment. But a didymochlaena will perish if the root ball dries out just once, so it needs constant attention to its needs. A high humidity level should be maintained all the time. In summer, or in a dry, centrally-heated atmosphere, twice daily spraying is essential. Spray all new fronds as soon as they unfold.

The unwieldy botanical name of *Didymochlaena truncatula* comes from two Greek and Latin words and means "a shortened double cloak."

A dull alcove can be transformed with a handsome, shade-loving cloak fern (*Didymochlaena truncatula*). But do not forget to mist the fern frequently to keep up the high levels of humidity it demands or the leaves will begin to turn brown.

SPORE PROPAGATION
This can be done from midsummer on
1 Snip off a ripe spore-laden frond, wrap it in a sheet of clean white paper and store it in a warm dry place. In a few days the frond will have shed its spores.
2 Thoroughly clean and then scald with boiling water the pot or container you propose to use as well as the drainage material. Fill the pot almost to the top with commercially available seed-raising mix. Sterilize this with boiling water. Immediately cover with glass.
3 Once the mix has cooled, spread the spores quickly, and evenly, over the surface. Immediately cover again.
4 Plunge the base of the container in boiled water. Drain. Keep the soil moist but never water from the top.
5 Leave containers in a shady, protected spot. A green film will appear on the surface followed by minute fronds.
6 Remove the cover. When plants are big enough to handle, transplant them.

GREEN THUMB GUIDE

Watering and feeding
Didymochlaena will appreciate frequent spraying with tepid, soft water. In the growing season spray as often as twice daily and water the roots generously. From fall onward, through winter keep it cooler and drier. Do not spray or feed in the dormant season. Even in periods of active growth feed sparingly.

Light and temperature
Shade, all the year round, will favor this plant. It loves warm, damp niches. Normal living room temperatures will suit it well, but refrain from positioning it centrally in the room. In winter aim for temperatures in the 57°F to 60°F range. If it is near a sunny window, shade it from intense light.

Soil
A humus-rich mixture, imitating the tropical forest floor that is the plant's natural habitat worldwide, will suit your didymochlaena best.

Philodendron
PHILODENDRON

Few plants offer as much variety in leaf shape as the many species of philodendron: heart-shaped, arrow-shaped and all shapes between, including some that are deeply lobed, are readily obtainable from good garden centers. You should be aware, however, that the leaves of young plants (and the young leaves of older plants, also) may not have the distinctive shape of the mature leaf.

The philodendron is decorative and youthfully green. To this many species add rich bronze or reddish tones on the undersides of their leaves. Its popularity is thus well deserved. Another highly popular plant, often marketed under the name of split-leaf philodendron (*Philodendron pertusum*) is not of the same species at all: commonly known as the Swiss cheese plant, its correct name is *Monstera deliciosa*. (See p. 50.)

Climbers

Most popular of the climbing philodendrons is the heart-leaf (*P. scandens*). Its heart-shaped leaves, some 4 inches in length and 3 inches wide, appear on 2-inch leafstalks. New leaves have the fresh bronze transparency that makes the plant so attractive. Usually sold as *P. oxycardium* or *P. cordatum*, it is one of the most dependable creepers.

The heart-leaf philodendron also looks well as a trailing rather than climbing plant. As a trailer, however, its leaves will not grow so large. Whichever way you grow it, pinch out the growing tips to make the plant more bushy.

Other climbers – all of which can produce aerial roots – include *P.* 'Burgundy', a slow climber that bears bright red new leaves, darkening to burgundy red on the underside in maturity. *P. melanochrysum*, the black-gold philodendron, is also a slow grower, but will reach 6 feet in time. Its distinguishing feature is a dark, even blackish-green, leaf glistening with pink and bearing pinkish green veins. These leaves, which reach some 2 feet in length and 9 inches in width, make it a showy and dramatic container plant. The plant's leaf stems are unusual too: up to 20 inches in length, they may be covered in wartlike growths.

From Columbia comes *P. erubescens*. With its arrow-shaped leaves – dark green on top and coppery-red beneath – it is an attractive plant, enhanced still further if it is allowed to flower. When it does so, red spathes form to surround creamy white upthrust spadices or flower sheathes (see opposite).

A philodendron with a tropical fernlike profile is *P. angustisectum*. It has broad oval leaves, some 15 inches long and 12 inches broad, cut into many segments.

Climbing philodendrons can easily be propa-

P. tuxtlanum, which comes from Mexico, is one of the most vigorous climbing philodendrons. With its large spade shaped leaves and thick stem, this handsome plant will flourish in a poorly lit entryhall as well as by a sunny window.

Large and dramatic flowering spadices may add interest to *P. bipinnatifidum*, *P. erubescens* and *P. tuxtlanum* but they do sap the plant's energy away from leaf production. If you want the plant to cover as much ground as possible, cut them out.

gated by taking cuttings from growing tips. Take 3- to 4-inch cuttings from just below a node (the point where a leaf or shoot joins the main stem). Cut off the tough older leaf and plant the shoot in a 3-inch pot filled with equal parts of damp peat moss and coarse sand. Enclose the pot in a clear plastic bag and leave it in bright, but filtered, light for three to four weeks. Then remove the bag and water, if necessary, just to moisten the soil.

Non-climbing philodendrons

Among the non-climbing species are *P. bipinnatifidum* (see p. 30) a native of Brazil. This "tree" philodendron can reach a height of 4 feet in a container. Its large, 10- to 12-lobed, deeply incised leaves can measure 15 inches, on leafstalks of a similar length. Among other non-climbers, seek out Wendland's philodendron (*P. wendlandii*) with 12- to 18-inch lance-shaped leaves in a rosette formation. The large saddle-leaved philodendron (*P. selloum*) also forms an attractive rosette of leaves. Non-climbing philodendrons are best grown from seed.

GREEN THUMB GUIDE

Watering and feeding
Philodendrons can be watered sparingly, except in their active growing season when they should be watered freely with lukewarm water. Keep the soil moist throughout the summer but do not let it get soggy.

Glossy leaves and good color will be achieved by frequent, light feeding. Fast-growing species will need once-weekly feeds; less vigorous species can be fed once every two weeks. Species that develop aerial roots will benefit from misting. Where roots are encouraged to grow on a moss totem pole, keep the moss moist at all times. Brown leaf tips are a warning that the root system is too dry.

If you want to check the growth of over-vigorous plants, keep them in a cooler spot, feed them less well and let them dry out a little between waterings.

Light and temperature
Direct sunlight will kill this otherwise tough plant. Bright but filtered light, or indirect light, will suit a philodendron well. Poor light will cause stems to lengthen, at the expense of the abundant leaf growth that gives this plant its charm. Temperature ranges match those of living room conditions. The lower limit is 55°F.

Soil and repotting
Philodendrons enjoy a light, loosely-packed soil mix. A mix of coarse leafmold, loam and sharp sand will do well. Granules of perlite will make the mix friable.

'Green emerald' (*Philodendron erubescens*). This hardy and vigorous plant from Columbia has showy, long, narrow green leaves, with coppery-red undersides. The leafstalks, too, are reddish. It may also produce flowers.

Philodendron binpinnatifidum comes from Brazil. The bold, glossy, 10- to 12-lobed leaves of this non-climbing philodendron are arranged in an informal rosette radiating from the growing point.

Close-ups on the leaves of *Philodendron erubescens* 'Red Emerald' (*above*) and the shiny, lush *Philodendron radiatum* (*right*).

A leaf with a broader span. *Philodendron eprinium*, like most other philodendrons, will tolerate fairly low light levels and can be placed well away from a window.

TRAINING AND SUPPORT

Any of the climbing philodendrons is liable to become straggly, untidy, or even unmanageable if it is not properly trained or supported. The simple devices for training and support illustrated and described here can be used for these and many other types of houseplants, including ivies, tradescantias, hoyas and jasmines.
1 A hoop of plastic-coated wire pressed firmly into the soil produces an interesting shape when the plant is encouraged to grow around it. Tie the stems loosely at intervals, if necessary, to keep the shape neat with green garden string.
2 Many climbing philodendrons have aerial roots. Any such species is ideal for training on a moss pole. If kept damp, the pole will provide the aerial roots with moisture and so help promote lush, vigorous leaf growth.
3 A trio of bamboo poles, or similar supports, makes the basis of a miniature trellis for training a houseplant. The stems can be trained up individual poles or laced horizontally between poles.

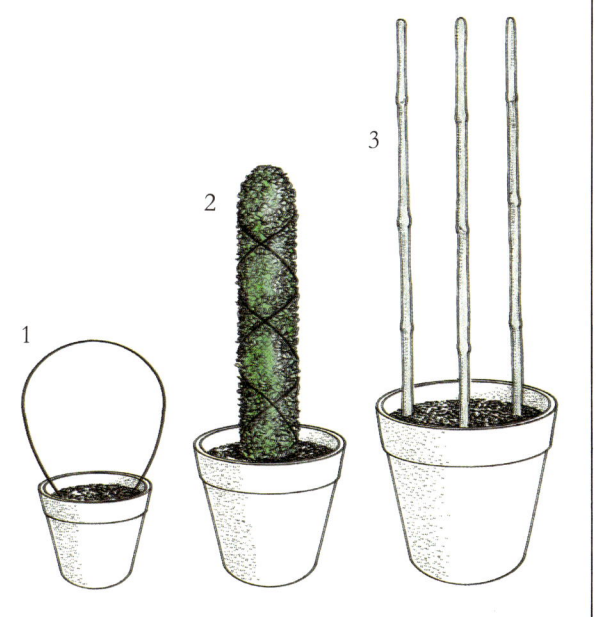

The familiar heart-shaped leaf of *Philodendron scandens*. Most popular and most widely sold of all the philodendrons, a single creeper of this species can grow as long as 50 feet. It can be trained to climb or to trail. Climbers produce larger leaves.

Norfolk Island pine
ARAUCARIA HETEROPHYLLA

The Christmas tree plant is another common name for this tiny conifer which is a highly popular substitute (where space is limited) for a full-size Christmas tree.

In its native Pacific island habitat off the coast of southern Australia it can reach a height of 200 feet on trunks some 9 feet across. As a houseplant it will not grow to more than around 4 feet, and that rather slowly, at around 6 inches a year.

In botanical terms, the Norfolk Island pine is classed not as a true pine but as an evergreen conifer. It is a sturdy survivor outdoors in milder climates, and so the cooler parts of the house are likely to suit it best. This pine is currently well favored by interior designers as an agreeable occupant of unheated hallways and conservatories. In warmer climate zones it will do well, container grown, in shady entryways.

An attractive feature of the pine is that it grows in tiered layers. Each year's new growth is marked by the fresh green hue of a new level of fan-shaped branches. These new needles will darken in color in the fall.

Even with the best of care, however a Norfolk Island pine will eventually lose its shape. As in the wild, lower branches will fall, spoiling the plant's symmetry.

To keep the plant at its best, repot it only at 4-year intervals. It likes to be potbound, and will reach its maximum height of about 48 inches in an 8-inch pot.

Although professional growers raise new specimens from seed, this is not an option for the home enthusiast, since the pot-grown pine will never bear you seed. Cuttings, however, will readily take root, but be aware that cuttings taken from side branches will develop as sideways pointing trees. While these may be just what is needed for a container display, they are unlikely to present attractively shaped specimens on their own.

Only a cutting taken from the growing tip of the parent plant will produce a new straight tree – but will, of course, at the same time sabotage the shape of the original plant. An alternative is to cut an older specimen to within 6 inches of its base from which it will send up new shoots. These can be cut and raised in a peat-and-sand mix to grow into straight new trees.

Propagation by air layering is also possible with this pine. Cut a growing branch half way through and prop the cut open with a matchstick. Dust the exposed area in hormone rooting powder then wrap round it a ball of damp sphagnum moss. Bind the ball with clear plastic and gather it in tightly top and bottom. In a few months new roots will form and push through the moss. Cut the stem just below these roots and plant as a new tree.

With care, a Norfolk Island pine will live for many years. Like a Christmas tree, however, it is liable to suffer from needle drop. This is likely to occur through an over-dry atmosphere, or because the plant is getting too little light.

GREEN THUMB GUIDE

Watering and feeding
Water liberally, if possible with soft, lime-free water, during the growing season. Make sure that the plant never becomes waterlogged. In the dormant period, when the plant is losing little moisture through its needles, restrict watering to just keeping the soil damp. Overwatering will cause the lower branches to fall. Hot dry air and drying out of the soil will have the same effect. In very hot weather mist the foliage.

Feed every two weeks in the growing season, with an acid-type fertilizer designed for rhododendrons.

Light and temperature
Medium light serves this tree best, and a site near a north-facing window is ideal. Never crowd this plant indoors; outdoors, in warmer zones, it will do well in the shade of larger trees. Indoors, the Norfolk Island pine will give warning that it is too far from the window when needles start to fall. The tree is generous in its temperature range tolerance: this makes it a good occupant of unheated hallways. It can bear temperatures between 45°F and 75°F. If the temperature exceeds 75°F spray the foliage more frequently.

Soil and repotting
Both loam and peat-based potting mixes will provide good mediums for growth. Professional growers may use equal parts peat moss and coarse sand, adding to each bucket of the mix $1\frac{1}{2}$ tablespoons superphosphate, 1 tablespoon ground limestone and 2 teaspoons of a general purpose fertilizer.

These small conifers can tolerate being potbound and will do well on repotting at 3- to 4-year intervals. If you wish to repot, do so in the spring.

An attractive profile and thickly-needled branches give the Norfolk pine a simple charm. At Christmas or on other festive occasions, the branches can be festooned with decorations.

"Miniature bamboo"
POGONATHERUM PANICEUM

It is often difficult for the non-botanist to tell how houseplants came by their Latin or Greek names. But in the case of *Pogonatherum* it is only too obvious once its derivation is explained. The Greek *pogon* meaning "beard" and *ather*, "bristle" are particularly apt for this dense, wild spiky plant strikingly reminiscent of a long-untended beard.

Bamboos are considered by experts in plant classification either as members of the grass family (Gramineae), or are separated off into their own family, the Bambusaceae. In fact, *Pogonatherum paniceum* is botanically exclusive, since it belongs to the Panicoideae, a sub-family of the Gramineae, which includes only three groups.

Its rigid, erect stalks, which grow between 6 and 24 inches long, are usually much branched in the upper part. From these grow narrow, needle-shaped leaves which are very similar in appearance to those of bamboo.

Older plants that are beginning to look uncomfortably dense should be cut back to get rid of old growth and allow the plant the chance to regain its youthful grace and vigor.

While the miniature bamboo can be propagated by seed, the speedier method of simple division is more likely to appeal to the indoor gardener.

GREEN THUMB GUIDE

Watering and feeding
P. paniceum needs generous watering during the active growing period from April through August. For the remainder of the year it should be watered moderately; let the top half inch of soil dry out between waterings.

The plant's nutritional requirements will be satisfied by an application of liquid fertilizer every two weeks during the growing period.

Light and temperature
Good light is essential, and the miniature bamboo will do well sited near a window.

During the summer months the plant will not object to standing outside, provided it is not subjected to excessive heat. In winter it will do well in a cool room.

Soil and repotting
A good standard soil-based potting mix enriched with leaf mold is recommended for this plant. It should be repotted annually in spring.

PROPAGATION BY DIVISION

This is the easiest of all methods of vegetative propagation, and is suitable for most plants that send up more than one stem from the roots. Notable exceptions are palms and all plants with woody stems. It should be done, ideally, at the beginning of the active growing period, which for most plants is the spring. In the case of flowering plants, divide when they are dormant. If they do not have a dormant period, divide them when they are at their least profuse.

In the case of Boston ferns (*Nephrolepis*, see p. 20) and asparagus ferns you should cut plant stems back to soil level before dividing.

Remove the plant from its pot and look for a point or points where division looks possible. In the case of a plant such as the African violet (*Saintpaulia*) which grows in several rosettes, it is easy to see where the division should be made. There are no guidelines about how many divisions to make, but it is obviously essential that each has its fair share of roots and stems.

It may help to shake or even wash off some of the old potting mix before attempting to pry the sections apart, but avoid this if you can for it is likely to damage the fine root hairs. If you cannot prise the divisions gently apart by hand, you will have to resort to a clean, sharp knife. This will almost certainly be necessary in the case of ferns with densely tangled roots or with tough rhizomes. If you can avoid cutting all the way through, using the knife to separate the clump initially and then completing the division by hand, so much the better.

Divisions should be planted in pots that are an inch or so wider across than their root ball, to leave room for growth. Study the root length and fill the pot with just enough mix to come up to the lowest root point. Then, holding the plant in position with one hand, trickle potting mix around it with the other. Tap the pot to get rid of air pockets before filling to its final level. If you are using a soil-based potting mix, make sure it is well tamped down around the newly divided plant.

Water well and then stand the plants in good indirect light until you are sure the operation has been successful. Then they can be treated as other plants in the species.

The miniature bamboo, native of China, Malaysia and northeast Australia has an unusual, spiky form that will make it the focal point in a room. In tropical regions it is cultivated as an ornamental for patios and verandas.

Eucalyptus
EUCALYPTUS

Undemanding and adaptable, the eucalyptus, is a fast-growing decorative indoor foliage plant native to Australia. It is also the most widely cultivated non-native tree in California and Arizona. It grows very tall very quickly so its long-term potential as a houseplant is somewhat limited.

Eucalyptus trees generally display two sorts of foliage: juvenile foliage which is soft and produces a variety of shapes, and mature foliage which is tougher and more regular in shape.

The Tasmanian blue gum (*E. globulus*) is one of the most popular indoor varieties. Its silvery green leaves, like those of most eucalyptus, contain a pungent and aromatic oil. When the tree is commercially grown this has a medicinal use. In spring the gum will produce small creamy white flowers. It can only be grown indoors for a couple of years, since it makes such vigorous growth – 3 to 4 feet per year. Its juvenile leaves are produced close to the main stem. Heart-shaped, they are greyish-blue with a white powdery texture.

The plant will branch quite naturally, but if you want to hold back its growth and extend the appearance of softer juvenile foliage, then prune it back hard for a couple of years. This will also make for a bushier and more attractive plant. When it grows too big for the average indoor situation transfer it to a warm site on a patio or sundeck. In severely cold conditions try storing it in a garage or basement. It will probably shed a few leaves in winter, but new spring growth will replace them.

The cider gum tree (*E. gunnii*) is probably the most sought after of indoor eucalypts since it is slower growing than most other species. In a container it will only increase 12 to 18 inches each year. Young shoots have a particularly attractive pinkish blush. It produces small creamy white flowers in spring and summer when mature.

Because of their swift growth eucalypts will need to be repotted frequently, in some cases twice a year. Make sure that the potting medium, usually a leaf mold enriched soil-based mix, completely covers the swollen root system of the plant.

Eucalyptus plants are easily raised from seed, which should be sown in spring in a moist soil-based mix. If possible, place seeds in a heated propagator tray. Otherwise keep them in a place where bright light and high temperatures, 70°F–75°F can be guaranteed. The seedlings will develop quickly – within 2 to 3 weeks the first pair of true leaves should have appeared. Plant them on into individual 3-inch pots and water them sparingly. As soon as the roots have filled the 3-inch pots, repot and treat them as adult plants.

Pinching out
Encourage bushy growth in a eucalyptus, or any houseplant liable to become straggly, by pinching out the tips of the longest shoots. The plant will thus be stimulated to sprout new side shoots from near the base of its stem.

> **GREEN THUMB GUIDE**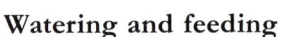
>
> **Watering and feeding**
> Even in the active growing period, *Eucalyptus globulus, will need only moderate watering. Remember that in its wild state it is one of the toughest and tallest trees in the world: to restrain it into the dimensions of a houseplant will need a degree of starvation. Make sure the potting mixture is thoroughly moistened when you do water. You can, however, allow up to the top third of the mixture in the container to dry out between waterings.*
>
> **Light and temperature**
> *Full sunlight, reminiscent of the native bush in Australia and Tasmania, is the ideal and the necessity for a eucalyptus. Leaves will quickly lose their color out of direct light. From Arizona to California, eucalypts are the most widely grown non-native trees.*
>
> **Soil**
> *Eucalyptus will grow well in a rich, soil-based potting mix. Some will not tolerate lime.*

The Tasmanian blue gum (*Eucalyptus globulus*) demands bright, direct sunlight. It will probably outstrip its indoor situation in a few years.

Introducing palms

Prized for their stately, elegant appearance in their natural tropical and subtropical habitats, members of the palm family (Palmae) can look just as imposing planted in avenues and colonnades. Since the late nineteenth century they have also enjoyed great popularity as houseplants, gracing the most elegant rooms. The luxuriant foliage of palms softens harsh angles and awkward corners and brings an exotic hint of the tropics to your home.

There are over 3,400 species of palm, many grown commercially for their products rather than simply as ornamentals. As houseplants they survive adequately attention.

In their natural habitats, palms bloom and fruit, and many grow as tall as 100 feet. Growth is made from the terminal bud, hidden inside the leaf clusters at the tip of the palm. If the growing point is damaged or destroyed, the plant will not grow and eventually dies. This point, or apical bud, is sought after as a culinary delicacy.

Indoor palms do not always resemble their outdoor relatives; their growth and development is inhibited by the size of the pots in which they are grown. Most indoor specimens will produce one or two new fronds a year, but they will not, of course, grow to the size they would outdoors.

The roots of palms are fibrous and, with sufficient nutrients, the root ball can survive in a small container. Growth in a palm takes place first in the girth of its trunk. Growth in height usually occurs only after the trunk has reached its maximum width. Palms in containers take longer to reach maximum girth and so can be grown successfully in small containers and rooms for many years. Most palms are single-stemmed but many produce offshoots, called suckers, from the base. These suckers can be removed to form new plants.

Each species of palm has a fixed number of leaves it can support at any one time. As old leaves fall and die they are replaced by new ones which develop at the crown. The plant will suffer no ill effects if you remove damaged leaves by cutting them from the trunk at their bases.

The most common leaf shapes are the fan, or palmate, and the feather, or pinnate (divided) leaf. Some pinnate leaves are bipinnate (doubly divided), like those of the caryotas or fishtail palms.

Palms are happiest in bright light and relative warmth. Avoid direct sunlight on indoor palms; it will scorch their leaves.

Plant more than one parlor palm in the same container to display this dwarf species to best advantage. The mini-forest created by its feathery fronds makes a screen to divide a large space.

Parlor palm
CHAMAEDOREA ELEGANS

The parlor, or good luck, palm is a pretty little palm with feathery leaves 18 to 24 inches long. This palm enjoys crowded living space. Plant it either with several of its own kind in the same container, or with small and varied specimens in a terrarium or dish garden. A slow-grower, it will take several years to reach its maximum indoor height of around 3 to 4 feet.

Although the parlor palm will tolerate dry air, it needs plenty of water in the growing season. But brown leaf tips warn that conditions may be too dry for the plant, and spindly leaves are a sure sign that it is starved of light. Watch out, too, for mottled yellow leaves revealing infestation by red spider mites. Regular spraying with tepid water should prevent such an outbreak. Fortunately, the parlor palm benefits from grooming: cut out dead or damaged leaves to display the healthy leaves that grow in pairs along the elegant stalks.

As a bonus, this delicate indoor plant may produce tiny yellow flowers and later orange fruit the size of peas.

Propagation is usually by seed and a difficult process for the amateur since a bottom heat of well over 70°F is needed for germination. If you want to try growing parlor palms from seed, sow three in the same small pot. When they germinate, prick them out carefully and plant them in individual pots. Take care to screen them from strong light while very young, and keep them warm and moist for the first few years of growth.

Repot parlor palms in spring, but only if the root ball completely fills the container. Handle roots with great care when repotting; they are especially sensitive and any damage will set back the plant's development. Older plants rarely need repotting.

A native of Mexico, the parlor palm does well indoors or as a patio plant in suitable climates.

GREEN THUMB GUIDE

Watering and feeding
Water as much as the plant demands during active growth. Keep the potting mix thoroughly moist: water can even remain in the base of the container if it rests on a bed of stones. In this way the plant's roots can absorb extra water as they need. Always maintain good drainage, however; moistness not wetness is the aim. In winter, when the plant is resting, allow the top two thirds of soil to dry out between waterings. Feed with liquid fertilizer at half strength every two weeks from spring through late summer.

Light and temperature
Bright, but filtered light is best for this palm. It does well at a north-facing window or toward the center of a room – positions few plants like. It prefers temperatures down to and around 50°F in its resting period and normal living room warmth at other times.

Soil and repotting
Use a standard potting mix, well firmed around the root ball. Repot every two or three years in spring, but only if the roots have filled the container.

In ideal conditions, the parlor palm produces clusters of tiny yellow flowers when one foot high.

Yellow palm
CHRYSALIDOCARPUS LUTESCENS

This feathery, elegant yellow palm comes from Madagascar where it is also called *Areca lutescens*. Its name yellow palm comes from the color of its long leaf stems. Borne on these are long, featherlike, pinnate fronds, which grow straight up in reedy clusters from the base of the leaf stems before arching gently downward. On a plant 5 feet tall the fronds are about 3 to 4 feet long. Growth is slow – the palm increases in height by only 6 to 8 inches each year. The stems of mature plants are marked with bamboolike notches – the scars of lost leaves.

When young and relatively small, these beautiful palms are graceful and pleasing wherever they are placed. They may well outgrow the available space, however, and since they cannot be pruned may have to be moved outdoors in frost-free zones, or found more spacious homes. Because of the potential size, choose a site for this palm where it can spread and grow for some years. It should not be in direct sunlight, nor in a place where its leaves will be knocked.

If you have seeds of this palm it is a slow but simple matter to germinate them. Sow in spring at a temperature of about 65°F. It takes some years for seed-grown plants to reach any reasonable size.

A more successful and faster means of increasing your stock of yellow palms is by using its suckers. In spring, while repotting the whole plant, remove any basal suckers. Take only suckers which are about 12 inches long and have established root growth. Plant the suckers in 4- or 5-inch pots in a mixture of two parts soil-based potting mix and one part coarse sand or lightly crushed perlite to encourage good root growth.

Place the pot inside a plastic bag to retain humidity and create a mini-hothouse. After six weeks in a warm room, remove the plastic bag and give the new plant a little water. Once it is established and showing some new growth, water as for a mature plant but do not feed for the first three months of growth. Then feed in the normal way. Repot sucker-grown plants in a standard potting mix the following spring.

The elegant feathery fronds of the yellow palm arch delicately at their highest point.

GREEN THUMB GUIDE

Watering and feeding
The yellow palm likes a moist soil but do not let its roots stand in water. If the temperature should fall below 55°F, give just enough water to prevent the soil from drying out completely. During the period of active growth (spring through summer), feed once a month with a liquid fertilizer. Do not feed this palm at other times of year.

Light and temperature
Sunlight filtered through window shades or drapes is best for this palm. It must have good indirect light, though, so find it a position away from the center of the room. By day it thrives in temperatures of 70°F to 80°F; at night 65°F to 70°F is suitable.

Soil and repotting
Use a soil-based mix for best results. Repot the parent plant every second spring until it has outgrown the largest containers – and, probably, available house space. When this happens, simply add a top dressing of fresh potting mix each year. To top dress, scrape a few inches of old potting mix from the top of the pot. Refill with new potting mix, adding a little fertilizer at the same time. Press the new soil firmly around the roots, but take care not to damage them. The pot size determines the growth rate. Not repotting will maintain size.

Fishtail palm
CARYOTA

The fishtail palm is slightly ragged in appearance, and more fern- than palmlike, but is nonetheless a popular houseplant. Two different species are grown: *Caryota mitis* and *Caryota urens*. *C. mitis* grows up to 8 feet tall indoors and has fronds carried on leafstalks 1 to 2 feet long. Their deliberate arch gives the plant a crownlike look.

The second species, *C. urens* also grows 8 feet tall indoors, but has leaflets with more geometric, less ragged shapes than those of *C. mitis*. In general, it is a smarter looking plant. It will not, however, survive temperatures below 32°F, so protect it from low night-time temperatures.

Both palms have gray-green leafstalks, bearing bipinnate (doubly divided) fronds which resemble fishtails in their shape. The fronds of mature plants are several feet long and wide, but growth is slow – only a few inches every year. Grown indoors, caryotas never produce flowers or fruits.

Mature caryotas thrive packed closely together in the same pot. Unlike other palms, grow them in pots that seem just a little too small. Only repot caryotas into larger containers when the plants are 2 to 3 years old, and then only when the plant is in the middle of a burst of growth.

The plants may suffer from infestations of red spider mites – brown leaf tips are a warning sign. Spray to eradicate the mites, but check also that the air is not dry for the palm since this, too, could cause the brown tips.

Propagate from seeds sown in spring at temperatures over 75°F. *C. mitis* can also be propagated by planting up the basal suckers. Plant the suckers in a potting mix and leave them in a warm room. Do not cover the plants, but see that light is filtered through a drape. Keep the new plants moist until growth is obvious, then water and care as for a mature plant.

The chunky, geometric fishtail palm (*Caryota*) makes an attractive addition to a well-lit, warm position.

GREEN THUMB GUIDE

Watering and feeding
Only give as much water as needed to keep the soil mixture just moist. Caryotas like humid conditions, so stand the container on a tray of damp pebbles to increase the humidity. When the plant does not seem to be making much new growth, allow the top third of the soil to dry out completely before watering. Feed with liquid fertilizer from spring through summer to encourage growth. Do not feed at other times of year.

Light and temperature
Warmth is the caryotas' main need. They will thrive at temperatures of 75°F to 80°F by day and 65°F to 70°F by night, and do not like temperatures below 55°F. In Southeast Asia, their natural home, caryotas grow in full sun. Indoors, they like as much light as possible, but strong direct light should be filtered through a light drape.

Soil and repotting
Use a standard potting mix for these palms and make sure the soil around the root ball is firmly pressed down. Once a plant has outgrown the largest available pot, simply top dress it in spring with new potting mix.

Coconut palm
COCOS NUCIFERA

The coconut shell, which bears three "eyes," reminded the Portuguese seamen who first found it in India of a rather unpleasantly grimacing face. Thus they used the Portuguese word *coco*, meaning a "distorted mask," to describe it.

The geographical origins of the coconut palm are a little obscure: different schools of thought favor either Polynesia or South America. Wherever it first came from, it is now one of the world's most useful and widely cultivated trees. It is found growing in all tropical regions, either as an ornamental tree or as an important economic crop.

The coconut palm is most commonly found growing on or near the sea shore and on islands. The sea has probably played a significant role in its distribution: the buoyant nuts have been known to be carried over 500 miles by ocean currents. Even after such a journey they still remain able to germinate.

There are three cultivated varieties of this palm. The most common is the giant coconut palm which can grow to 100 feet. This is the one that, in the popular imagination, conjures pictures of sun-drenched tropical beaches.

The coconut palm's cylindrical stem, like that of other palms (but unlike that of most other trees) hardly tapers. It is surmounted by a crown of featherlike leaves which may grow to 20 feet in length. Their heaviness belies their feathery appearance: they can each weigh as much as 30 pounds. The palm's small white flowers take about twelve months to develop into the fruits that appear in bunches of between twelve and twenty. The fruits are the familiar hard-shelled coconuts which are enclosed in a gray-brown, elliptical three-sided envelope. The fibrous layer which lies between the smooth outer shell and the hard shell protecting the kernel is sold as "coir," used for making ropes and coconut matting.

Low growing varieties, the 'Dwarf Gold Malay' and 'Dwarf Samoan' abound in Indonesia, Malaya and parts of Polynesia. Both produce large clusters of nuts which, when mature, have yellow outer shells.

The versatile palm
The white meaty flesh of the coconut is the part most familiar to consumers outside tropical countries; coconut oil, milk and cream also feature very largely in tropical cuisine. Oil is extracted from the dried white flesh or "copra," which is also used in the manufacture of margarine.

The juice tapped from the trunk before and during the flowering period is fermented to give a highly potent palm wine. And the ripening fruits themselves, from the eighth month of their growth onward, yield a refreshing and nourishing drink. (By the time exported nuts have reached their destination, the coconut "milk" has, unfortunately, lost much of its original sweetness and freshness.) The hard shells of the coconut may also be halved and hollowed and used to fashion ladles as well as other domestic utensils. The palm leaves are woven into thatches for roofs and the trunks themselves are used both in furniture making and building.
Other useful palms include the sugar palm (*Arenga pinnata*) which, like the coconut, is used in its entirety. The sugar is tapped and may be fermented to make palm wine. The sugar is sought after for use in Southeast Asian and Indian cookery.

GREEN THUMB GUIDE

Watering and feeding
Once the coconut has sprouted keep the fibrous shell and the soil-based potting mix moist. When the plant is about 24 inches high, water the soil but not the exposed shell and fibers. The palm's root will plunge to the bottom of the container, so make sure that your watering penetrates to that level.

During the first year of growth the palm will not need a liquid fertilizer. It should derive sufficient nutrients from the soil and from the nut itself. In the second year a standard liquid fertilizer applied twice a week during the growing period will benefit the plant greatly.

Light and temperature
A favorite of the sun, the coconut palm will flourish in all warm zones given moisture at the roots and plenty of sunlight. In cooler climes beware putting leaves that are used to filtered sunlight into direct sun – they will burn. The minimum winter temperatures for this palm are 61°F to 64°F. In summer you could move it to a balcony or patio but protect the leaves from wind and bright sun until adjusted.

Soil
A soil-based mix, blended with one third quantity of coarse sand or perlite is the best match to the coconut's natural foothold on tropical beaches and oases.

Growing a coconut palm indoors
Many garden centers sell coconuts with shoots and a first pair of leaves already formed. It is also possible to raise your own palm providing you can obtain a coconut with its outer shell and interior fibers intact.
1 With a sharp knife, cut away a 2- to 2½-inch slice from the shell over the eye of the coconut, where it was attached to the parent plant. This cut should expose the porous fibers on the inside.
2 Immerse the nut for a few hours in a solution of one teaspoon of household salt in two pints of water. Make sure the incision is below water level, so that the fibers absorb the solution.
3 Cover the base of a suitably large container with a layer of drainage material and then partially fill with a good soil-based potting mix. Set the nut in the soil, with its top third projecting and the exposed fibers uppermost so they can be watered. Keep moist and at between 76°F and 82°F.
4 After three or four weeks, the first shoots will appear. They will open into a pair of large, spoon-shaped leaves and, from their first appearance, will need plenty of light. Continue to water the exposed fibers until the nut develops a root system.
5 The fast-growing palm will reach 3 feet within a year and within three years will probably have outgrown the space allotted to it.

Date palm
PHOENIX DACTYLIFERA

Sun-drenched oases in the Middle East and North Africa are the exotic origins of the feathery date palm, *Phoenix dactylifera*. Known the world over as the classic palm of Palm Springs golf course, and of all movie oases sets, it can grow to 80 feet or more in its natural habitat, or where it is cultivated outdoors. It has a slender trunk with waxy grayish leaves. The leaflets are pointed and stiff.

The date palm is, however, a popular choice as an indoor palm and its ornamental presence will give pleasure provided it has space to dominate. It is a relatively slow-growing palm so it will be manageable for some years.

The plant produces suckers at its base which can be propagated if you wish, but it enjoys growing in thick clumps in its native habitat, so leave a few to grow in the same pot. It is hardy to temperatures as low as 20°F when its leaves will die.

The Canary date palm (*Phoenix canariensis*) is a hardy and popular species originating from the Canary Islands, off Africa. It also thrives in Madeira and on the Mediterranean coast where it grows to

GREEN THUMB GUIDE

Watering and feeding
Date palms should be watered sparingly during their winter rest period. Keep the soil mix just moist. When active growth begins again increase the amount of water, so that the mix is well-moistened but do not overwater: never allow the plant's roots to stand in water. Date palms will benefit from regular feeding – every two weeks – during the growing season, from the beginning of spring through the end of summer. Do not feed them at other times of the year.

Light and temperature
Date palms are satisfied with the steady temperature of a normally warm room. Ideal day temperatures for them are 75°F to 80°F and at night they prefer a range from 65°F to 70°F. In winter they will benefit from a rest period at temperatures as low as 50°F to 55°F. They are hardy to 20°F but at lower temperatures leaves will be killed. Generally slow-growing, date palms will flourish in bright but indirect or curtain-filtered light. They will tolerate full sunlight well, also.

Soil and repotting
Date palms grow well in peat-based mixes: one third peat, one third vermiculite (absorbent mica particles) with one third coarse sand or ground volcanic material (perlite).

If mature plants seem crowded in their pots, repot during spring activity.

Turn your living room into an indoor oasis with a date palm (*Phoenix dactylifera*). A flourishing specimen such as this certainly produces a dramatic effect. This palm is especially successful on patios or sundecks of seaside or desert gardens.

50 feet. In optimum climatic conditions outdoors, it will reach 60 feet, but it is slow-growing until its trunk is formed, then it speeds ahead. Young plants do well in pots and tubs for many years and it is a popular choice for many public places including hotel lobbies, restaurants and offices. It is ideal for home-growing indoors and out – on the patio or sundeck in warmer zones.

The head of the Canary date palm is composed of a number of gracefully arching fronds; the bright green leaf bases are covered with wispy fibrous hairs. If kept in a small container it will reach 6 feet; its elegant dark green fronds will hang in sweeps of 3 feet.

Because of its hardy nature this palm will grow in poor light, unfavorable temperatures and with minimum care. However, if conditions are more favorable it will thrive, becoming a dramatic focal point of any room. The only drawback is that its fronds are stiff and hard, so position it where it will not scrape anyone. However, if it is grown indoors constantly the fronds will become softer. Remove any old or dead leaves with a saw. If not treated in this way it would be some years before the leaves would eventually fall off. Apart from a neatening effect, the saw will produce an attractive diamond-shape pattern on the stem. The Canary date palm is hardy down to temperatures of 20°F. If frost-damaged it will be slow to develop new foliage.

The miniature date palm (*Phoenix roebelinii*) is probably the palm most widely grown in containers indoors. A native of Vietnam, this palm has fine fronds which form a thickly arching crown. It is usually single-stemmed but sometimes several occur. If you prefer to keep it single-stemmed simply take out the young stems as they appear. This palm will grow to about 6 feet and requires more moisture than other container-grown species. It does best in bright, filtered light. Dark corners will not suit this small palm. But it will tolerate periods of relatively low light levels. Under these conditions, however, growth will be halted and the palm will not thrive. It is best kept out of drafts, since its leaf tips may become brown.

Fine roots growing on the surface of the soil are an indication that it is time to repot. Do this, if possible, when active growth in spring is about to take place. Transfer the plant to a pot 2 inches larger, but be careful not to damage the root system. When the date palm has outgrown the largest container you have, simply top dress rather than repot. Most date palms benefit from repotting every two or three years; older plants should only be repotted every three to five years. Use a potting mix enriched with leaf mold, mixed with coarse sand or perlite.

Its stiff, spiky fronds make the popular Canary date palm (*Phoenix canariensis*) a plant that needs thoughtful placement. If grown in low light levels for a number of years, its fronds will lose their hardness, giving the whole plant a softer look.

Elegant feathery fronds combined with small dimensions make the pigmy date palm (*Phoenix roebelinii*) a popular choice in a wide range of situations. It will tolerate low light levels, but will grow much faster in a good, bright light.

Desert fan palm
WASHINGTONIA FILIFERA

The desert fan or petticoat palm (*Washingtonia filifera*) is a handsome plant, with dramatic fan-shaped leaves. Popular in California and other warm areas for planting outdoors, it is adaptable and can tolerate a wide range of environments. It can even survive temperatures as low as 50°F. As a houseplant, it presents few problems and will thrive with proper care and attention.

Like all palms, the desert fan grows from one terminal bud at the tip of the stem which must always be treated with great care. If this bud, or apical point, is destroyed or damaged no more leaves can grow and the entire plant will die.

The elegant fronds of *W. filifera* spread out like open fans and can be 2 feet or more across. The leaves are gray-green and borne on spiny green leafstalks, 18 inches or so long. Fine fibers hang from the edges of the leaf divisions.

A similar variety is the thread, or Mexican fan, palm (*W. robusta*). A taller plant than the desert fan, it is faster growing and has bright-green leaves. The segments of these leaves are much stiffer and less deeply cut than those of its relative.

These decorative plants look good wherever they are displayed, but basket containers complement their luxuriant greenery particularly well. Choose a basket large enough for the plant's pot to fit comfortably inside and place a masonite-backed cork pad under the basket to protect the floor or table from any water seeping through from the pot.

Both the desert fan and thread palm can only be propagated from seed at temperatures of at least 80°F. This is a difficult process, requiring special equipment, and best left to professionals.

GREEN THUMB GUIDE

Watering and feeding
Throughout the active growing period, water this palm generously. Make sure the potting mix is kept thoroughly moist, particularly if the plant is placed near a sunny window. In winter, keep the soil slightly moist, but let the top half inch dry out before watering. Feed with liquid fertilizer every two weeks throughout the active growing period.

Light and temperature
Both these palms need bright light throughout the year, ideally with several hours of sunshine each day. Although happier in warm, or even hot, rooms, they will tolerate temperatures down to 50°F. Mist spray the plants if they are in a heated room.

Soil and repotting
Use a soil-based mix, adding one third rotted leaf mold or peat moss to help it retain moisture. Repot only when the plant seems pot-bound.

The elegant desert fan (*Washingtonia filifera*) has dramatic fan-shaped leaves. The nutlike object on its stem is a new leaf about to unfurl.

Screw pine
PANDANUS VEITCHII

Popular for its ornamental foliage, the screw pine (*Pandanus veitchii*) has a rosette of leaves, rather like a giant pineapple, and a corkscrew like trunk. It is a Polynesian plant and a member of the Pandanaceae family, which contains some 650 species of tropical evergreen shrubs.

The screw pine's dark green leaves are striped, and sometimes edged, with white or cream, and barbed with fine, sharp teeth. A mature plant of six to eight years old may be up to 4 feet tall, with a spread of 3 feet, and have leaves 3 feet long and 3 inches wide. Another variety, *P. veitchii* 'Compacta' is smaller and more bushy, as its name suggests. Its leaves are 15 to 24 inches long and up to 2 inches wide.

When about two or three years old, the screw pine begins to produce aerial roots about half an inch thick. These appear from below the lower leaves of the plant and grow downward to take root in the potting mix, making stiltlike props that support the trunk.

Use any suckers that appear at the base of the screw pine for propagating new plants. Wait until the suckers have developed leaves 6 to 8 inches long, before cutting them off the parent plant. Plant them in a moistened mixture of peat moss and coarse sand and cover the pot with a plastic bag to retain humidity. Keep it in a warm place, preferably at a temperature of about 75°F.

Four to six weeks later the suckers should have rooted. Remove the plastic bag for longer periods each day to give the new plant a chance gradually to acclimatize to a drier atmosphere, then treat it as a mature specimen.

The screw pine (*Pandanus veitchii*) has broad green leaves, striped with white or cream. Unlike many houseplants, it thrives in a sunny position.

GREEN THUMB GUIDE

Watering and feeding
Always use tepid water for the screw pine. During the active growth period, spring through summer, water liberally but do not leave the plant standing in water. Allow the soil to become partially dry between waterings. In the winter rest period, water more sparingly. Mist the foliage in warm weather or place the plant outside in a summer shower. Feed with a standard liquid fertilizer every two weeks during the active growth period.

Light and temperature
P. veitchii needs overall bright light and, if possible, should receive at least three hours of direct sunshine daily. Normal room temperature is fine, but it should not fall below 55°F. Avoid leaving the plant in too dry an atmosphere or the edges and tips of its leaves will turn brown. To keep humidity high, stand the plant on a tray filled with moist pebbles.

Soil and repotting
Repot in spring to a pot one size larger, until the plant outgrows the largest container available. The stiltlike aerial roots may tend to push the base of the screw pine upward. If this happens, top dress the plant with fresh soil to cover any roots exposed during the active growth period.

Sago plant
CYCAS REVOLUTA

The oldest known seed-bearing plant on earth, the sago plant (*Cycas revoluta*) has only recently become popular as a houseplant. It comes from China and Japan and is now a protected species in areas where it grows wild. Although its name is derived from the Greek word "Kykas," meaning palm, it is not in fact related to that family, but is a member of the Cycadaceae family.

The cylindrical trunk of the sago plant grows to a height of no more than 3 or 4 inches. Stiff stalks grow from this trunk, and bear equally stiff leaves that arch 2 or 3 feet outward. These leaves are dark green with lighter undersides. Sponge them from time to time to keep them free of dust. Considerable patience is needed to rear this plant successfully – it grows very slowly and a new leaf can take as long as two years to develop.

The sago plant is probably seen at its best grown in the warm steamy conditions of botanic gardens. In favorable climates, where winter temperatures do not go below 50°F, it can also be grown outside.

To propagate this plant, use the woody growth knobs at the trunk and leaf bases. Remove and allow the cuttings to dry out for a few days, then plant them in a peaty potting mix. The sago plant can also be grown from seed, but this is a tricky process, requiring temperatures over 80°F to ensure germination and growth.

The sago plant is an extremely ancient species and fossils of it have been found in some of the oldest geological formations on earth. Placed in a suitable container to complement its stiff, dark-green leaves, it makes an attractive display indoors or out on a patio or terrace.

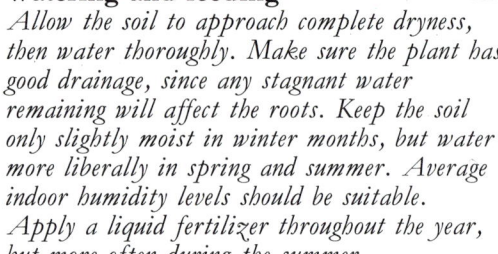

GREEN THUMB GUIDE

Watering and feeding
Allow the soil to approach complete dryness, then water thoroughly. Make sure the plant has good drainage, since any stagnant water remaining will affect the roots. Keep the soil only slightly moist in winter months, but water more liberally in spring and summer. Average indoor humidity levels should be suitable. Apply a liquid fertilizer throughout the year, but more often during the summer.

Light and temperature
Grown outdoors, the sago plant likes sheltered, slightly shady positions. Indoors, avoid placing it in direct sunlight which will burn its leaves and turn them brown. If this should happen, pick off the affected leaves. Keep the plant in average room temperature of 60°F to 65°F.

Soil and repotting
Repot only when pot-bound. Use a good peaty potting mix.

House holly
CYRTOMIUM FALCATUM

One of the most tolerant of all ferns, house holly, or fishtail fern, is also one of the longest lived. It is a member of the Polypodiaceae family, and a native of Japan, China and South Africa. Although a slow-growing plant, it will eventually reach a height of about 2 feet. Small leaves 3 to 5 inches long and 1 to 2 inches wide make up its fronds. These leaves are dark, glossy green and resemble holly leaves without the spines – hence the plant's common name.

A new and increasingly popular way of displaying such ferns is the fern wall – a glass case, containing a variety of ferns from temperate zones. Ideally, the glass case should have a sloping roof to allow the condensed moisture to run down the sides.

To plant a fern wall, first fill the bottom of the case with drainage material, such as charcoal, then add a layer of peat and finally a quantity of potting mix. Water the soil moderately and allow it to settle. Plant a selection of ferns. Holly fern, sword fern and maidenhair fern are all good choices, but add any others you like that suit the conditions. A few small pebbles placed among the ferns adds to the decorative effect of the display.

Propagate the holly fern in spring by dividing overcrowded clumps. Make sure you use only older specimens.

GREEN THUMB GUIDE

Watering and feeding
During the active growing period, from April through August, water the plant liberally and mist frequently. Water sparingly at other times of the year, but never let the soil dry out. Take particular care not to overwater if the temperature falls below 55°F. Feed with liquid fertilizer every two weeks during the growing period.

Light and temperature
Protect the holly fern from direct sunlight, which will make its fronds pale and cause scorch marks on their surfaces. It does, however, need good indirect light since poor light affects its growth adversely. The temperature should not fall below 50°F; 60°F to 70°F is ideal.

Soil and repotting
Repot in spring when the fronds fill the old pot. Use a mixture of equal parts of peat and soil-based potting mix.

Although an extremely tolerant houseplant, the holly fern should be protected from direct sunlight. Its shiny, green, holly-shaped leaves are its main attraction, but these may eventually show signs of age and discoloration. If this should happen, wait until spring and cut the damaged leaves away. New leaves will grow and the plant will regain its freshness and beauty.

Swiss cheese plant
MONSTERA DELICIOSA

This native of the Mexican tropical forests has become one of the most popular houseplants. It is certainly one of the most decorative, with its huge, glossy, deeply slashed evergreen leaves. In favorable conditions and in a suitably large container monstera may grow to 20 feet or more tall and 6 to 8 feet wide.

Also known as the Mexican breadfruit plant or the Swiss cheese plant, *Monstera deliciosa* is sometimes mistakenly sold as the split-leaf philodendron, *Philodendron pertusum* or *Monstera pertusum*. The confusion arises because the oval leaves of young plants look very similar to those of certain philodendrons. As with philodendrons, the distinctive shape is only evident in mature leaves.

Plants which have grown too straggly and lost their lower leaves will gain a new lease on life from air-layering, which should be done in the spring or summer. Using a sharp knife, cut out two rings half an inch apart on the stem, then peel off the bark and brush the stripped area with hormone rooting powder.

Wrap a rectangular piece of plastic sheeting around the stem, tying it tightly at the bottom with string, leaving the top open. Fill the plastic "receptacle" with moistened sphagnum moss, then close and secure the top.

Within six to eight weeks, the roots should

Monsteras grow so vigorously that they may need extra room, like this specimen.

appear through the moss. When they do, remove the plastic and cut the stem below the roots. Pot the new root ball in potting mix together with the moss to avoid damaging the roots. Make sure that the pot used is one inch larger than the root ball.

In a mature plant, leaves that refuse to produce those essential holes may be suffering from underfeeding, too little water, cold or lack of light. If the upper leaves have no holes, push the aerial roots well down into the soil, or allow them to grow into the moist support provided by a totem pole.

Yellowing, wilting leaves are a sign of overwatering. If there is no wilting or rotting, underfeeding is likely to be the cause. Dry air will make the leaves go brown and papery at the edges. Mist the leaves and surround the pot with damp peat.

Leggy growth and pale, small leaves are likely to result from too shady a position. Brown spots along the veins on the underside of the leaves may be caused by the red spider mite. If so, apply a systemic insecticide.

GREEN THUMB GUIDE

Watering and feeding
Do not overwater, since this causes the roots to rot. During the winter keep the soil just moist, but during the spring and summer water liberally, allowing the soil to become dryish between waterings. Spray often, since large amounts of water evaporate from the leaves. During the active growth period from April through September, apply a standard liquid fertilizer once every two weeks.

Light and temperature
It is essential to keep the plant out of direct sunlight during the active growing period. If you wish to keep it near a window, make sure that it is not south-facing. Monstera will do best in filtered (not deep) shade or in a moderately bright situation. Normal room temperatures are suitable. Increase humidity above 70°F and do not expose to less than 50°F. Active growth starts at 65°F.

Soil
Monstera prefers a free-draining potting mix containing a good proportion of both peat and coarse sand or vermiculite and perlite. Many ready-made peat-based mixes are suitable.

When grown in a conservatory or greenhouse monstera may produce lilylike flowers. These have a half-oval, creamy white spathe with a thick spadix 10 inches long in the center. The spadix develops into a white, edible fruit which may look unappetizing but tastes like a cross between a pineapple and banana.

MAKING A TOTEM POLE

A moss-covered totem pole is an ideal way to support a monstera and provide it with moisture.
1 Bind a thick layer of damp sphagnum moss onto a wooden stake or hollow plastic tube using green plastic-covered wire.
2 Secure the moss with extra criss-crossed wires. Trim off any straggling pieces.

3 Bond the pole to the base of a pot with plaster of Paris. Fill the pot with potting mix, add the plant and train the aerial roots around the pole so that they can absorb moisture. Make sure the moss is kept moist at all times.

Elephant-foot plant
BEAUCARNEA RECURVATA

The unusual elephant-foot plant, or ponytail palm (*Beaucarnea recurvata*), is a striking plant. Its common names suggest its appearance: its trunk is like that of a palm, but the more mature specimens have a greatly swollen base, resembling an elephant's foot. A cluster of long narrow, green leaves, its "ponytail," arches out from the top of the trunk.

A member of the Agavaceae family, this plant originates from the southern parts of Mexico and the highlands of Guatemala, where it can grow to more than 30 feet tall. In its native habitat, it is exposed to intense burning sunlight and long periods without rain. Like all succulents, it survives these harsh conditions because it can store water in its trunk; this enables it to stay alive through times of drought. Grown indoors, it rarely exceeds a height of more than 6 to 8 feet, even in the most favorable conditions.

In the wild, small white flowers appear in groups at the top of the elephant-foot tree, but as a houseplant it seldom flowers. Provided it is treated well, however, it will be long lived and become increasingly attractive as it matures.

Its furrowed bark and elephantine, swollen base give the plant a strong, sculptural outline. As such, it is ideal used as a focal point, positioned against a plain, pale-colored background. Place the plant in a south-facing aspect if possible – it does best in full sun. In the right spot and in a container that complements its structure, a large elephant-foot plant can look extremely striking.

Although the plant can be propagated by taking offsets at repotting time, this is a tricky process and it may be better to buy new plants. If you do decide to propagate by offsets, take them from a fairly mature plant. Using a sharp knife or razor blade, cut the offset as near as possible to the main stem of the plant. Prepare a rooting mix made up of equal parts of peat moss, perlite, and vermiculite or coarse sand. Make sure that the prepared mixture is sterile and that it retains moisture without becoming waterlogged.

Push the base of the offset firmly into the mixture which should be slightly moist, but not sodden. Keep it in a temperature of between 65°F and 75°F, in a strong light but not direct sun. Once sufficient rooting shows, transfer the plant to another pot, containing standard potting mix, and treat it in the same way as an adult plant.

Like other succulents, the elephant-foot plant is prone to attack by mealy bugs and root mealy bugs which cause its leaves to discolor and attack its roots respectively. Treat both with an insecticide.

GREEN THUMB GUIDE

Watering and feeding
Since it is a succulent, the elephant-foot plant can survive on its own resources if faced with a water shortage. Do not let this be a reason for neglecting and underwatering the plant, however. Water thoroughly in spring and summer, letting the soil become moderately dry before watering again. Water less often in winter. There is no need to mist the plant. During the active growing period (April through August), give the plant liquid fertilizer every two weeks.

Light and temperature
The plant can be placed on a windowsill in hot direct sunshine. To avoid its growth becoming distorted and top leaves discoloring, rotate the plant daily so that all of it receives the benefit of the sun's rays in turn. It will be happy in the warmth of an average living room, but in winter the temperature should not drop below 50°F.

Soil and repotting
Use a soil-based mix, but add a quantity of coarse sand or perlite. Repot young plants every second year, and older specimens every third year.

Although the elephant-foot plant is a rather strange-looking palm, it does have its own special charm. At home in the scorching sun of southern Mexico and Guatemala, it nevertheless makes a fine and striking houseplant in the right setting. It will do well in full sun all year round.

Cardamom
ELETTARIA CARDAMOMUM

One satisfaction of keeping this many-stemmed plant is that its vigorous leafy growth demands division of the plant each spring, to create new specimens of a useful and adaptable houseplant.

The cardamom, in its natural home in such Far Eastern countries as Java, bears a fruit which the Romans once valued at its own weight in gold, and on which the Spaniards of the 1500s built a spice trade. Today, as one of the newer houseplants on the market, the cardamom will not bear spicy fruits but it has the special value that it will thrive in poor light where few other plants would survive and it has wonderfully scented foliage.

The cardamom grows to a height of some $2\frac{1}{2}$ feet, and bears long, narrow, pointed-oval leaves on thick stems that spring from a creeping rhizome (root tuber). If grown in a greenhouse, shorter stems sprouting from the rhizome may, in spring, bear the plant's white-striped pink blooms. Indoors, however, it flowers only rarely. Side shoots bearing new foliage growth are numerous, quickly giving the plant a characteristically crowded appearance in its container.

Instead of repotting you can simply top dress the soil. However, if this is difficult because there are so many stems in the container, then divide the plant and repot individual new plants. To do this, remove the whole plant from the container and separate the stems carefully so that no damage is done. Try to keep the rhizomes and fibrous roots intact. Pot up in a humus-rich loam-based mix and care for it as you would a mature plant.

GREEN THUMB GUIDE

Watering and feeding
The cardamom is not a demanding plant; it needs only moderate amounts of water during its growing period and a minimum amount in the resting period. Just sufficient water to stop the potting mix drying out will be suitable. A standard liquid fertilizer, applied once every two weeks, will provide adequate feeding during its period of active growth.

Light and temperature
The cardamom is tolerant of almost all light conditions except for direct sunlight, which explains its new-found popularity as a houseplant. Medium or bright but filtered light will suit it best. But it can also cope well with poor light conditions. The temperature range it prefers is that of normal living room conditions. Below 55°F there is a risk that some leaves will go brown at the edges. Direct sunlight will have the same effect.

Soil
A standard potting mix or a mix of equal parts of humus, peat moss and perlite will serve this plant well.

Plant division
An easy and also inexpensive way to increase cardamoms is by simple division.
1 Carefully remove the plant from its pot, shake off any excess soil, then either pull away a small piece of the plant or carefully slice it off with a sharp knife, making sure each stem is joined to a sizeable root.
2 Pot up each clump in a small pot filled with rooting mix placed over broken crocks. Tap the pot against the side of a table several times as you fill it to settle the soil.

54

As a houseplant, *Elettaria cardamomum* will thrive even in poor light conditions, putting forth a profusion of lush, bright-green leaves. Cardamom seeds play an important role in Indian cuisine.

Stenochlaena
STENOCHLAENA TENUIFOLIA

The fern *Stenochlaena tenuifolia* is a native of India, Malaysia and South Africa, where it grows as a climber on the trunks of palm trees. Its name, *Stenochlaena*, means *stenos*, narrow, and *chlaina*, cloak, which gives a clue to its appearance. It has some resemblance to the holly fern (*Cyrtomium falcatum*), and is a member of the same family (Polypodiaceae).

Elegant fronds extend 3 to 5 feet from the main stem and may be 12 to 18 inches wide. Their long, pointed leaflets are 6 to 9 inches long and shiny green in color. The climbing rhizomes are woody and brown, with a slightly scaly look.

This graceful plant can be placed alone or used as part of a staged display with other plants of different sizes. To arrange a staged display, place different varieties of plants on, say, upturned flowerpots to give additional height. Place smaller plants in front of the raised plants to hide their bases and create a lush bank of varied but harmonizing foliage.

Propagate this plant in early spring, using a section of rhizome from an older plant. Ideally, the section used should have 2 or 3 inches of root. Plant the roots just below the surface of a 3-inch pot filled with well-moistened standard potting mix.

If a rhizome section without roots is used, pot it and cover the whole pot with a plastic bag. The mini-hothouse this creates encourages the rhizome to root. Place the plant in bright, filtered light and keep the soil barely moist until some growth appears. Thereafter treat as a mature plant.

GREEN THUMB GUIDE

Watering and feeding
S. tenuifolia needs regular, moderate watering, but allow the top half-inch of soil to dry out between waterings. The plant will survive occasional periods without water. Use lime-free water and in summer place the plant outside occasionally to be refreshed by showers of rain. In winter, provided the plant is kept warm, restricted watering is sufficient. Mist the plant regularly. During the active growing period, feed with liquid fertilizer every two weeks.

Light and temperature
Position the plant in sunlight or bright filtered light. Too much sunshine can scorch the fronds and turn them pale. A temperature of 60°F to 70°F is ideal and 50°F is the absolute minimum.

Soil and repotting
Use a standard potting mix. Repot in spring when the roots fill the pot.

With its elegant, dark-green leaves, *Stenochlaena tenuifolia* is a charming, luxuriant plant that will enhance any home. It is equally effective on its own or as part of a display with other plants.

Schefflera

SCHEFFLERA ARBORICOLA, SCHEFFLERA ACTINOPHYLLA

The two easy-to-grow, long-lived plants, *Schefflera arboricola* and *S. actinophylla*, are both members of the Araliaceae (ivy) family. Both are named after the German botanist J. C. Scheffler, but their descriptions are sometimes preceded by the name *Brassaia*.

S. arboricola is the more popular of the two species – it demands less light than its relative and is not susceptible to spider mites. A native of Asia, it is particularly common in Taiwan. In the wild it may reach a height of 20 feet with a spread of 10 feet and produces flowers shaped like flattened spheres. These blooms are yellow at first, gradually turning to glowing bronze. Indoors, it grows to between 5 and 6 feet high. Its decorative fingered leaves each bear six to ten leaflets of up to 3 inches long. As it matures, *S. arboricola* develops a solid base, and growth from this area will tolerate severe pruning. Use any stems taken from the base of the plant for air layering.

In Australia, New Guinea and Java where it grows wild, *S. actinophylla* reaches a towering 100 feet and produces a riot of magnificent scarlet flowers. As a houseplant it will grow up to 6 feet tall, so needs plenty of room, but it does not flower when grown indoors. This species is well worth growing, however, for its tough, shiny foliage which bursts forth from a central point – an arrangement which gives the plant its common names of Queensland umbrella tree and starleaf. The olive-green, oval-shaped leaflets are shiny and leathery and, on a mature plant, can be up to 12 inches long and 3 inches wide. Each is borne on its own short stalk.

Schefflera plants have elegant fans of leaves that create beautiful displays in any living area. They can stand on their own in colorful containers, or be grouped with other plants such as the weeping fig (*Ficus benjamina*), the spineless yucca (*Yucca elephantipes*), or the rare and beautiful silk oak (*Grevillia robusta*). A display of such size and range requires considerable room, but is quite breathtaking. Whether using your plant alone or with others, experiment with different positions to be sure of using it to best effect.

Air layering

Propagate scheffl28eras by growing them from seed or by air layering. Raising plants from seed is difficult. A tray with bottom heat is required for inducing germination, and this process may be best left to the professionals.

To propagate by air layering, select a stem, cut out two rings half an inch apart and then peel off the bark. Apply hormone rooting powder to the stripped area, wrap a piece of plastic sheet around the stem and secure it at the base. Fill the cuplike container made by the bag with moistened sphagnum moss and tie securely at the top with string or a twist tie.

A few weeks later white roots should appear on the outside of the moss. Cut the stem off the parent plant just below the ball of moss. Transfer the new root ball to a pot large enough to accommodate sufficient potting mix to keep the new plant firmly held. Care for the new plant as for an older specimen.

GREEN THUMB GUIDE

Watering and feeding
Water moderately during the active growing period (spring through summer). Allow the potting mix to dry out partially between waterings, then moisten thoroughly. During the winter rest period, provide just enough water to keep the soil from drying out completely. Mist both species of schefflera frequently, and sponge the leaves to free them of dust. In the growing season, apply a liquid fertilizer every two weeks.

Light and temperature
Keep scheffleras out of direct sunshine but in good light. S. arboricola in particular, will tolerate a little shade but must have sufficient light in winter or its top shoots will dry out. Scheffleras are happiest in temperatures between 60°F and 65°F; below 55°F their leaves have a tendency to drop.

Soil and repotting
Repot scheffleras once a year to a pot one size larger. When plants reach maximum pot size, simply top dress the soil, using standard potting mix.

The arching stalks of *Schefflera actinophylla* resemble the framework of an umbrella – hence its common name of umbrella tree.

Perhaps the most popular of the schefflera because it tolerates some shade, *Schefflera arboricola* has fine, shiny foliage, and makes a pleasing display.

Jacaranda
JACARANDA MIMOSIFOLIA

In their native Brazil, and in other subtropical climates, jacarandas are small flowering deciduous trees that can grow to a height of 30 feet. In April they produce a cloud of blue blossoms of breathtaking beauty. The flowers bloom on bare twigs and the leaves only appear when the flowering is over.

Jacarandas belong to the Bignoniaceae family. *Jacaranda mimosifolia* is the only species that will adapt to an indoor climate and grow as a houseplant. It will not flower indoors, but in ideal greenhouse or conservatory conditions it will produce beautiful clusters of lavender-blue tubular flowers.

As a houseplant, jacaranda is prized for its elegant, lacy foliage, and in a good environment it will reach a height of 3 feet. Plants are not always readily available, but once you have one you will find it is not difficult to grow, provided it is sited in a sunny room. It will look well on a pedestal, framed by a window as in our photograph, or alongside other plants with contrasting foliage.

The jacaranda is single-stemmed when young, but when it reaches a height of 2 feet, several stems branch off. It will keep its delicate, mimosalike leaves throughout the winter if conditions are right.

You can give a lanky, straggly plant a new look by pruning it severely in the spring. Cut back some of the older stems with a sharp knife and new shoots will eventually appear, giving the plant a bushier more shapely look. A less severe method of pruning is to pinch out the growing tip of the plant. This induces it to put out new shoots and, in due course, these too can be pinched out.

Jacarandas are best grown from seed, which can be obtained from many mail-order seed companies. The best time to plant is in February or March. Before sowing, soak the hard-coated seeds in water for twenty-four hours to soften them. Be sure to use a sowing and rooting mix, not the standard potting mix that will be used once the seedlings are established. The sowing mix must be sterilized, to lessen the risk of damping-off seedlings. Keep the mix barely moist. Germination should occur in two to three weeks. When the seedlings reach a height of 6 to 8 inches they can be transferred to 4- or 5-inch pots filled with standard potting mix.

Jacarandas can be repotted each spring in pots two sizes larger, up to a maximum of about 10 inches. Since older plants are less attractive, new ones should be raised at least every other year, or stem cuttings taken.

GREEN THUMB GUIDE

Watering and feeding
Jacarandas should be watered with tepid lime-free water or with rainwater. During the spring and summer, in the active growth period, the plant should be watered moderately. Give it just enough to moisten the potting mix thoroughly. Allow the top half of the mix to dry out before watering again. In the winter water sparingly, to prevent the mix from drying out. A lack of humidity will cause the leaves to dry up and shrivel, so mist them frequently, particularly if the plant is near a radiator.

Light and temperature
While jacarandas like bright light, they should not be exposed to direct sunlight for more than three hours a day, particularly in the summer. Ideal positions would be in south-, east- or west-facing windows.

Jacarandas will do well in an average or slightly above average room temperature and will tolerate a temperature as low as 45°F.

Soil and repotting
Use a standard potting mix.

Jacarandas can be moved on each spring to a pot two sizes larger until a maximum of about 10 inches has been reached. Top dress once a year by gently removing the top inch or so of old soil mix and refilling with fresh mix to which you have added a little fertilizer.

Flowering jacaranda trees produce a cloud of blue blossom. Indoor plants do not flower, but are prized for their lacy foliage.

Yucca
YUCCA ELEPHANTIPES

Yucca elephantipes, also known as the spineless yucca or palm lily, is a native of Mexico, but it is widely cultivated in Guatemala and neighboring countries. Since the end of the 1970s its worldwide popularity as a houseplant has created a minor industry in Central America. *Y. elephantipes* is a member of the agave family and is also closely related to the lilies. Another variety is *Y. alofolia* or *Y. gloriosa*, sometimes called Spanish bayonet, which has extremely sharp pointed leaves. Avoid bumping into them, as they can puncture the skin and cause nasty abrasions.

In its native habitat the yucca plant can grow to a height of 30 feet or more in harsh, desolate terrain where its fleshy roots search widely for water. For indoor cultivation, lengths of stems or trunks measuring up to 6 feet (these are waxed at the end where green leaves will ultimately sprout), are imported from Central America. On arrival, the stems (unwaxed ends) are placed in moist soil to induce rooting and this will occur after a period of six to eight weeks.

Eventually, pliant, lance-shaped, dark-green leaves appear at the top of the stem or trunk. A mature yucca has swordlike leaves and, after a period of several years, the plant may develop white, bell-shaped flowers, although this does not often occur outside its natural surroundings.

Yucca elephantipes is an expensive houseplant: its price is normally determined by its height and by the amount of foliage it produces. Since it is a rather unconventional plant in appearance, it is often chosen because its graphic shapes make an ideal focal point in a living room, an office reception area or an atrium.

Mature specimens of the yucca occasionally produce new plantlets or side shoots (usually at the base of the stem or trunk) and these can be used for propagation. They should be cut off from the parent plant and placed in a pot containing a standard potting mix. Restrict watering so that the soil is barely moist.

Yucca seeds for planting indoors are available, but the chances of their germinating are rather limited. If you decide to try, keep the seeds in a dark warm place after planting, but watch them closely because once they germinate and seedlings appear they must be brought into good light.

Because of a buildup of soluble fertilizer salts, the tips of yucca leaves may turn brown. To remedy this, flush the soil at least three times, each time letting the water drain away completely.

GREEN THUMB GUIDE

Watering and feeding
During the growing season (spring through fall) water thoroughly, but allow the soil to dry out considerably before the next watering. Water sparingly during the winter rest period, especially if the plant is grown in a cool room. Since the yucca can store water in its bulky stem, it can survive short periods of drought. It is important that the soil is not kept constantly wet, since the roots of the plant are sensitive to excessive water. Misting is not necessary. Fertilize with liquid fertilizer three times a year: spring, midsummer and early fall.

Light and temperature
In its native habitat the yucca is used to intensely strong sunlight, but it can do equally well in semi-shade. It will grow best if it is positioned by a south-facing window. In the summer it can be put out on a balcony or in a half shaded spot in the garden, but remember leaves that have grown indoors cannot stand direct sunlight outside. During the winter it will need an unheated and well-lit spot. The yucca will tolerate room temperatures of between 60°F to 65°F during the summer period and 50°F to 55°F throughout the winter.

Soil and repotting
Larger, older plants can be repotted every two years in the spring. Be careful with the plant's thick, strong roots when repotting and use a stable pot that is broad and low. Use a standard potting mix that is well drained.

Yucca elephantipes is grown in Central America from where stems cut to lengths of about 6 feet are exported throughout the world. The crown of the stem produces swordlike leaves while the stem itself remains dormant.

Plants for cool rooms

As well as the plants described in the preceding pages, there are many other excellent green foliage plants. Because certain indoor environments may pose specific, temperature-related problems, the plants have been divided into those showing preference for cool, temperate or warm rooms.

The plants suggested for cooler rooms prefer a maximum temperature of about 55°F, minimum 45°F. They range from the shiny, bright-green leaves of the Chinese fan palm (*Livistona chinensis*) to the dark-green, silky foliage of the silk oak (*Grevillea robusta*). The hardy and undemanding cast iron plant (*Aspidistra elatior*) is the most obvious candidate of all for a cool room.

AUSTRALIAN LAUREL
Pittosporum tobira
A native of China and Japan, this plant can grow up to 5 feet. Its thick, glossy leaves are arranged in whorls around much-branching stems. In the summer months it produces tubular white or pale yellow flowers that have a fragrance like orange blossom.

Green thumb guide
Water plentifully while in active growth, moderately during the rest period. Use a liquid fertilizer every two weeks during the active growth period.

Prefers bright light with at least three hours of direct sunlight daily. Normal room temperatures, except in winter when plants should be rested at 50°F.

Use a standard potting mix and repot every spring in a larger pot.

CAST IRON PLANT
Aspidistra elatoir
This undemanding plant gets its common name from the cast iron constitution which enabled it to survive in the cold, and often fume-filled parlors and saloons of our great grandparents' days. Its dark-green leathery leaves grow to some 12 inches in length.

Green thumb guide
Water moderately throughout the year, allowing the top two thirds of the potting mix to dry out between waterings. Apply a liquid fertilizer every two weeks during the active growth period.

Prefers a medium light and will accept warm and cold conditions but not direct sunlight.

A standard potting mix is best. Repotting should be done only every 4 to 5 years in the spring.

CHINESE FAN PALM
Livistona chinensis
This splendid palm can eventually grow to 10 feet tall. The fan-shaped, bright-green leaves are 2 feet long and 2 feet wide with pointed segments.

Green thumb guide
Water moderately so that the potting mix is moist and let the top half inch of the soil dry out between waterings. Feed actively growing plants with a liquid fertilizer every two weeks.

Provide moderate light but not direct sunlight and normal room temperatures, with a minimum of 45°F.

Use a standard potting mix; only repot when the plant shows signs of becoming potbound.

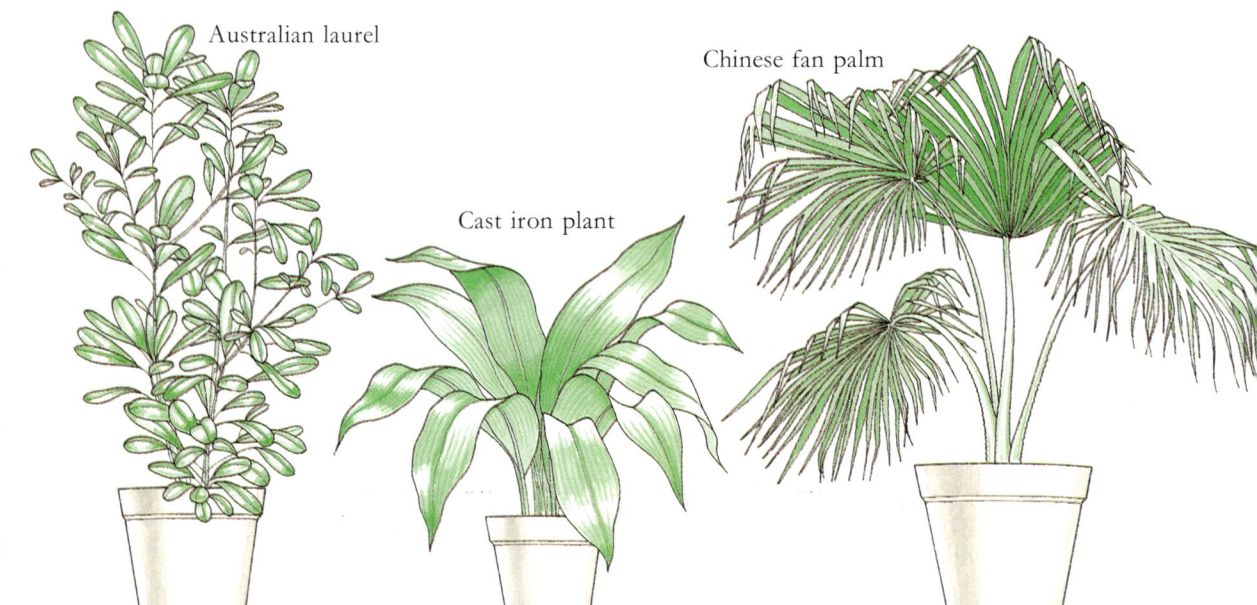

Australian laurel

Cast iron plant

Chinese fan palm

LADY PALM
Rhapis excelsa

Originating from the high-altitude forests of China, this plant can grow to 5 feet tall indoors. It has fan-shaped, dark-green leaves cut lengthwise into a number of separate segments. They grow at the end of thin, arching stems along a brown, hairy main trunk.

Green thumb guide

Apply moderate amounts of water when growth is active. Water sparingly during the rest period. Feed growing plants with liquid fertilizer once a month.

Grow in bright filtered light, but in winter give three to four hours of direct sunlight daily. Normal room temperatures, with a minimum of about 45°F.

Use a standard potting mix and repot into larger pots no more than once in two years.

PIGGYBACK PLANT
Tolmiea menziesii

Natives of the west coast of North America, piggyback plants are ideal for cool rooms or unheated porches. They get their common name from the plantlets which form at the base of mature leaves. They grow to a height of 12 inches, have bright-green leaves and are ideal for hanging baskets.

Green thumb guide

Water moderately in the summer and in the winter just enough to avoid the mixture drying out. Use a liquid fertilizer every two weeks when in active growth.

They can tolerate bright or medium light but will also grow in shade. Normal room temperatures are acceptable, above 50°F.

Use a standard potting mix. Repot at any time of the year. Older plants should not be repotted more than twice.

ROSE GERANIUM
Pelargonium graveolens

Indoors this pelargonium is grown for its perfumed leaves rather than its flowers. It will grow to 2 or 3 feet tall, has deeply fingered leaves with a rosy fragrance and spotted pink flowers.

Green thumb guide

Water moderately from spring through fall and sparingly in the winter. Feed a high-potassium liquid fertilizer every two weeks to actively growing plants.

Bright with some direct sunlight. Normal room temperature with a winter low of about 50°F.

Use a standard potting mix. Repot young plants in the spring.

SILK OAK
Grevillea robusta

In Western Australia the silk oak can grow to a height of 150 feet. As a houseplant it can grow to 6 feet tall within two to three years. It is an impressive evergreen with finely-divided leaves, resembling the fronds of a fern, tinged coppery-red and with silky white hair when young.

Green thumb guide

Water liberally from spring through fall, allowing the top half of the soil to dry out before watering again. When plants are growing rapidly, feed with a liquid fertilizer every two weeks.

Will accept direct sunlight but will grow in medium light too. Keep in the brightest possible spot in the winter. Normal room temperatures during the active growth period but not less than 45°F in the winter.

Grevilleas prefer a lime-free potting mix. Because of their vigorous growth, repot into a pot two sizes larger every spring.

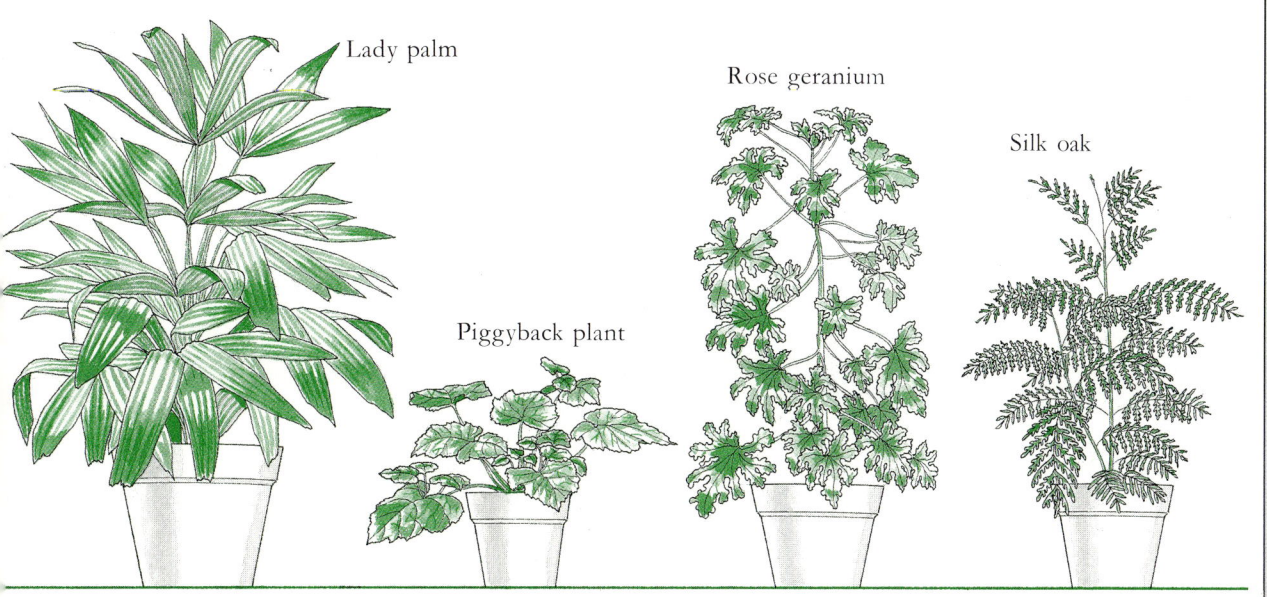

Lady palm

Piggyback plant

Rose geranium

Silk oak

Plants for temperate rooms

A wide range of plants will thrive in temperate conditions. These include some that need bright light as well as those that are happier in medium light or partial shade. Among those suggested here, the houseplants which prefer bright light are: the Chinese loquat (*Eriobtrya japonica*), a small indoor tree with broad olive-green leaves; the chestnut vine (*Tetrastigma voinieranum*), a fast-growing climber with large, toothed leaves; and the lace asparagus fern which is often added to bridal or florist bouquets.

Lovers of medium light include the button fern (*Pellaea rotundifolia*), a most unusual fern with numerous rounded pinnae; and the low bulrush (*Scirpus cernuus*). ("Temperate" means between 55°F and 65°F.)

CHINESE LOQUAT
Eriobotrya japonica
This small evergreen tree may grow between 8 and 10 feet tall indoors. The olive-green leaves are 10 inches long and 3 inches wide.

Green thumb guide
Water generously in the active growth period. At other times only water to prevent the mix drying out. Use a liquid fertilizer every two weeks when growth is active.

Prefers bright light and normal room temperatures above 50°F.

Use a standard potting mix and repot in a larger pot every spring.

CHRISTMAS FERN
Polystichum acrostichoides
Chosen for Christmas decorations, this plant has glossy, dark-green fronds that grow to 2 feet long.

Green thumb guide
Water plentifully during the growth period and keep the soil just moist in the winter. Apply a liquid fertilizer monthly from April through September.

Keep the plant in medium to bright light all year long. Average room temperatures but not less than 50°F in the winter.

Use a standard potting mix. Repot in the spring to a pot one size larger.

CLUB MOSS
Selaginella martensii
This plant has 12 inch long stems and fleshy, glistening, medium-green leaves supported on its stilt-like roots. Selaginellas were highly popular in Victorian times. They are good bottle garden subjects.

Green thumb guide
Water plentifully throughout the year. Feed with one quarter-strength liquid fertilizer every two weeks during the active growth period.

Stand in medium light throughout the year. Average room temperature with a winter low of 50°F to 55°F.

Use $\frac{2}{3}$ peat-based potting mix and $\frac{1}{3}$ coarse sand. Repot every spring into a larger pot.

DEER'S FOOT FERN
Davallia canariensis
A fern noted for its furry rhizomes which creep down over the pot (see also squirrel's foot fern, p. 24). It has medium green fronds about $1\frac{1}{2}$ feet long and 1 foot wide. It is an ideal plant for inclusion in a hanging basket.

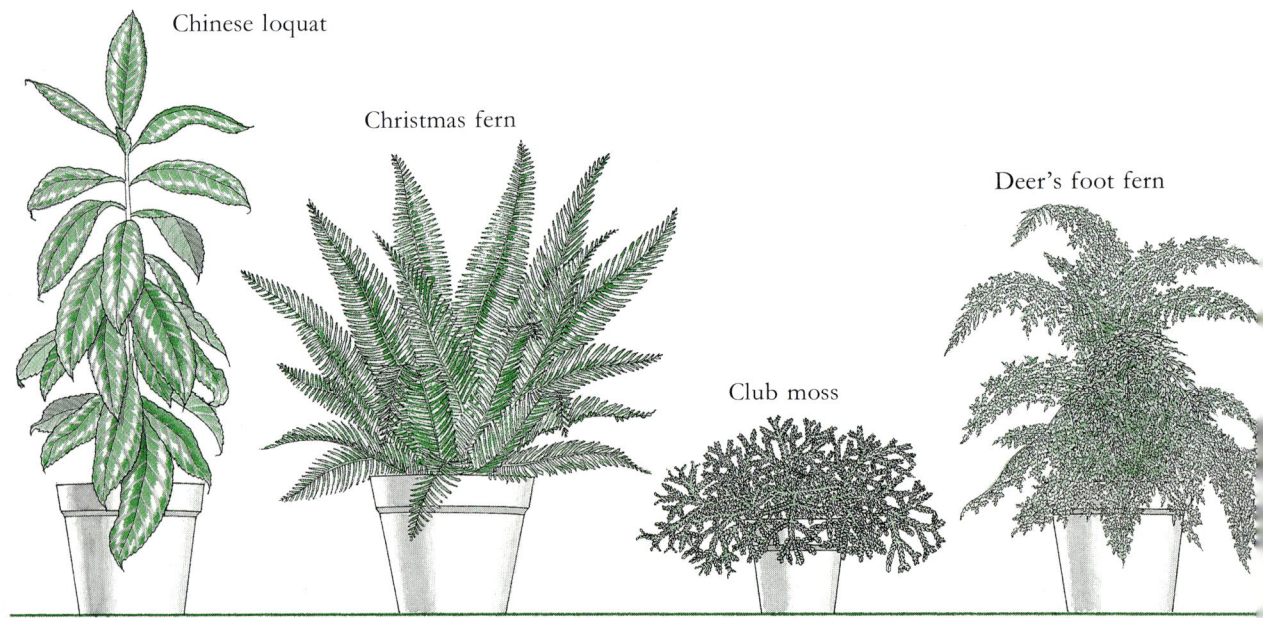
Chinese loquat
Christmas fern
Club moss
Deer's foot fern

Green thumb guide
Water moderately, allowing the mix to dry out a little between waterings. Feed every two weeks when growth is active.

Medium light and average room temperatures above 55°F.

Use equal parts of peat-based and soil-based mix. Repot in the spring.

CHESTNUT VINE
Tetrastigma voinieranum
This imposing plant can grow to 6 feet tall. Its leaves are glossy, dark olive-green above and have soft brown hair below.

Green thumb guide
Water moderately during active growth and less in the winter. Apply a liquid fertilizer every two weeks from April through August.

Bright light but avoid direct sunlight. Normal room temperatures.

Use a standard potting mix and repot to a pot two sizes larger each spring.

LACE ASPARAGUS FERN
Asparagus setaceus (formerly A. plumosus)
This fern's erect stems have flattened bright-green branchlets and can grow to 4 feet high.

Green thumb guide
Water liberally during the active growth period. Do not allow the soil to dry out in the winter. Apply a liquid fertilizer every two weeks from April through August.

Bright light but not direct sunlight. Normal room temperatures with a minimum of 55°F.

Use a standard potting mix and repot every spring into a pot one size larger.

BUTTON FERN
Pellaea rotundifolia
Although its arching, trailing habit is reminiscent of many ferns, the button fern's rounded pinnae look far from fernlike. The fronds may grow to about 12 inches in length and 1½ inches in width.

Green thumb guide
Water generously so the mixture is thoroughly moist. Reduce watering in the winter. Feed with a liquid fertilizer every two weeks from March through September.

Keep in medium light and in normal room temperatures but do not expose to less than 50°F.

Use a peat-based mix in a shallow container. Repot to a pot one size larger when growth becomes cramped.

HART'S TONGUE
Phyllitis scolopendrium
This fern has straplike 1 foot long fresh green fronds which rise from a branching rhizome.

Green thumb guide
Water moderately at all times but give less in the cool months. Feed a liquid fertilizer every two weeks during the active growing period.

Medium light throughout the year. Normal room temperature but not below 50°F.

Use a standard potting mix. Repot when the roots fill the pot.

LOW BULRUSH
Scirpus cernuus
This plant has shaggy stringlike leaves that grow 10 inches long. Each carries a tiny white flower.

Green thumb guide
The potting mix must be kept constantly moist. The plant will even tolerate standing permanently in water. Feed monthly during the active growth period.

Site in medium light. Will tolerate a temperature above 55°F throughout the year.

Use a standard potting mix. Repot when tufted growths cover the entire surface of the soil.

Chestnut vine — Lace asparagus fern — Button fern — Hart's tongue fern — Low bulrush

Plants for warm rooms

Many houseplants originally came from the tropics where they were adapted to survive high levels of heat and also of humidity. It thus is essential, in hot, dry, centrally-heated atmospheres to take special measures to ensure that the plants' needs are catered for.

Electric humidifiers are one of the most reliable methods of dealing with the problem of dry air. Grouping plants also maintains the humidity level to some extent. Misting, standing pots on a bed of irrigated pebbles or plunging them in larger containers filled with constantly damp peat moss are all effective alternatives.

BLECHNUM
Blechnum gibbum
This popular fern with its glossy, slightly drooping fronds has a palmlike profile. Its fronds grow up to 3 feet long and 1 foot wide and in time, crown a black trunk 3 feet tall. Blechnum will tolerate a slightly drier atmosphere than most ferns.

Green thumb guide
Water generously during the growing period and moderately in the winter. Feed every two weeks with half-strength liquid fertilizer during active growth.

Bright light but not direct sunlight is most suitable. This plant will tolerate a temperature slightly above 75°F with an average of 60°F in the winter.

Use standard potting mix. Repot every two years into a pot one size larger.

TOUCH-ME-NOT
Mimosa pudica
This fascinating plant has highly sensitive leaves that fold up at the slightest touch and then regain their normal shape within half an hour. It can grow to 20 inches tall indoors and its stems produce clusters of mauve-pink flowers with ideal conditions.

Green thumb guide
Water moderately to keep the potting mix moist at all times. Apply a high-potash liquid fertilizer once every two weeks.

Bright light is needed and in the summer it must have at least three hours of direct sunlight daily. Normal room temperatures but not less than 60°F in the winter.

Use a standard potting mix. Repot when roots appear through the drainage holes in the base of the pot.

IVY-LEAVED PEPEROMIA
Peperomia griseoargentea
There are many species of peperomia. This one is bushy with heart-shaped, grayish-green leaves that have a metallic sheen. It grows 6 inches tall and has greenish-white flower spikes on reddish stems that are 8 to 10 inches in length.

Green thumb guide
Water sparingly at all times and avoid wetting leaves and stems. A high level of humidity is needed. Apply half-strength liquid fertilizer every month from mid-spring through the fall.

A brightly lit site is best. Will thrive in normal room temperatures with a minimum of 55°F.

Use a standard potting mix. Young plants need repotting in the spring into a pot one size larger.

Blechnum

Ivy-leaved peperomia

Touch-me-not

"Do it yourself" plants

Adults and children alike find rearing new plants from the seeds or pits of fruit they have eaten an enjoyable and satisfying experience.

Although plants grown in this way are unlikely ever to produce fruit, simply seeing foliage emerge and grow is usually sufficient reward. The pits or seeds of oranges, lemons, dates, lychees and, of course, avocados all lend themselves to this sort of experimentation. Patience will be necessary, particularly in the case of date pits which may take three months to germinate.

For quicker results, the sprouting tops of vegetables such as carrots, parsnips and beets can be planted.

PINEAPPLE
Ananas comosus

Without removing the foliage, cut the top half inch or so off the pineapple fruit. Remove all the flesh from this "crown," leaving only the outer skin. Let it dry out over a couple of weeks, on a sunny windowsill if possible. When the crown is completely dry set it in a mix of coarse sand and peat.

Green thumb guide

Water enough to keep the potting mix moist throughout, allowing the top half to dry out between waterings. Use a liquid fertilizer every two weeks.

Bright light is essential and do not allow the temperature to fall below 64°F at night.

Use a lime-free, soil-based mixture and peat moss. Young plants need to be moved into a pot one size larger every spring.

CARROT
Daucus carota

This vegetable has a delightful ferny foliage. There are various ways it can be grown. Cut the top inch from a fresh carrot and stand it, cut end down, in a saucer of water. The carrot will soon sprout. Alternatively, pot up the top of the carrot, having removed all but the central leaves. The leaves will eventually yellow, when the plant should be discarded.

Green thumb guide

Top up the saucer regularly to prevent drying out, or keep potting mix moist at all times.

Place the plant in full sunlight and ensure a temperature above 50°F at all times.

Use a mixture of peat and sand, or pot the carrot in regular potting compost. Repotting should not be necessary.

SWEET POTATO VINE
Ipomoea batatas

Chose a potato that shows signs of sprouting. Then remove all but one or two shoots from the tuber before it is planted in a good quality potting mix. It will grow quite quickly into an attractive plant with heart-shaped leaves. It can then be encouraged either to climb or to trail.

Green thumb guide

Water liberally during the spring and summer but only sparingly in the winter.

Sweet potatoes need good light and normal room temperatures. Do not let the temperature fall below 55°F.

Repot in spring. Any new tubers that develop can be used to propagate new plants, or you can propagate by cuttings.

Sweet potato

Pineapple

Carrot

Index of Latin names

A
Adiantum 18, 19
  capillus-veneris 19
  cuneatum 18, 19
  hispidulum 19
  raddianum 18, 19
    – 'Decorum' 19
    – 'Fragrantissimum' 19
    – 'Fritz-Luthii' 19
  tenerum 19
    – 'Farleyense' 19
    – 'Wrightii' 19
Araucaria heterophylla 32
Areca lutescens 40
Arenga pinnata 43
Asparagus plumosus 67
  setaceus 67
Aspidistra elatior 64
Asplenium bulbiferum 18, 22, 23
  nidus 18, 23

B
Beaucarnea recurvata 52
Brassaia actinophylla see *Schefflera actinophylla*

C
Caryota mitis 41
  urens 41
Chamaedorea elegans 39
Chrysalidocarpus lutescens 40
Cocos nucifera 42
  – 'Dwarf Gold Malay' 42
  – 'Dwarf Samoan' 42
Cycas revoluta 48
Cyperus 4
  alternifolius 4
    – 'Gracilis' 4
  papyrus 4
Cyrtomium falcatum 49, 56

D
Davallia 18, 24
  bullata see *D. trichomanoides*
  canariensis 24, 66
  fejeensis 24
  mariesii see *D. trichomanoides*
  trichomanoides 24
Didymochlaena truncatula 27

E
Elettaria cardamomum 54, 55
Eriobtrya japonica 66
Eucalyptus globulus 36, 37
  gunnii 36

F
Fatsia japonica 14
Ficus 6–12
  australis 9
  benghalensis 6, 9
  benjamina 6, 10, 11, 57
    – 'Krishnae' 9
  buxifolia 11
  deltoidea 11
  diversifolia see *F. deltoidea*
  elastica 6
    – 'Robusta' 7
    – 'Schrijveriana' 7
  leprieurii 11
  lyrata 8
  macrophylla 7
  microcarpa 11
  nitida 11
  pumila 6, 12
    – 'Variegata' 6
  radicans see *F. sagittata*
    – 'Variegata' 13
  retusa 11
  rubiginosa 9
  sagittata 7, 13
    – 'Variegata' 9
  triangularis 11
  wildemaniana 9

G
Grevillea robusta 57, 64, 65

H
Hevea brasiliensis 6

J
Jacaranda mimosifolia 60

L
Livistona chinensis 64

M
Monstera deliciosa 28, 50, 51
Myrtus communis 16

N
Nephrolepis 20–21
  cordifolia 20
  exaltata 20, 21
  bostoniensis 20, 34
    – 'Rooseveltii' 20
    – 'Whitmanii' 20

P
Pandanus veitchii 47
  'Compacta' 47
Pelargonium graveolens 65
Pallaea rotundifolia 66, 67
Philodendron 28–31, 50
  angustisectum 28
  bipinnatifidum 28, 30
  'Burgundy' 28
  cordatum 28
  eprinium 30
  erubescens 28, 30
  melanochrysum 28
  oxycardium 28
  pertusum see *Monstera deliciosa*
  radiatum 30
  scandens 28, 31
  selloum 28
  tuxtla 28
  wendlandii 28
Phoenix 44–45
  canariensis 44, 45
  dactylifera 44
  roebelenii 45
Phyllitis scolopendrium 67
Pittosporum tobira 64
Platycerium bifurcatum 25
Pogonatherum paniceum 34
Polystichum acrostichoides 66
Pteris cretica 26
  – 'Albolineata' 26
  ensiformis 26
  – 'Victoriae' 26
  tremula 26

R
Rhapis excelsa 65

S
Saintpaulia 34
Schefflera actinophylla 57, 58
  arboricola 57, 59
Scirpus cernuus 67
Selaginella martensii 66
Stenochlaena tenuifolia 56

T
Tetrastigma voinieranum 66, 67

W
Washingtonia filifera 46
  robusta 46

Y
Yucca aloifolia 62
  elephantipes 57, 62, 63
  gloriosa 62

FAMILIES

A
Agavaceae 52
Araceae 28, 62
Araliaceae 57

B
Bambusaceae 34
Bignoniaceae 60

G
Gramineae 34

M
Moraceae 6
Myrtaceae 16

P
Palmae 38
Panicoideae 34
Polypodiaceae 49, 56

Index of English names

B
Bamboo, 'Miniature' 34
Banyan tree 6
Bulrush, low 67

C
Cardamom 54
Cast iron plant 64
Cider gum tree 36
Cretan brake 26

E
Elephant-foot plant 52, 53
Eucalyptus 36, 37

F
Fern, Australian maidenhair 19
  bird's nest 18, 23
  Boston 20, 34
  brittle maidenhair 18, 19
  button 66, 67
  Christmas 66
  cloak 27
  deer's foot 24, 66
  delta maidenhair 18, 19
  erect sword 20
  fan maidenhair 19
  fishtail 49
  glory 19
  hare's foot 24
  hart's tongue 67
  holly 49, 56
  lace asparagus 66, 67
  mother 18, 22
  Queen's 26
  rabbit's foot 24
  ribbon 26
  squirrel's foot 24
  staghorn 25
  sword 20, 21, 49
  Venus hair 19
  Victoria 26
Fig 6–12
  Bengal 9
  Chinese 12
  creeping 6, 12
  fiddle-leaf 8
  mistletoe 11
  moreton bay 7
  rusty 9
  weeping 6, 10, 57

G
Geranium, rose 65

J
Jacaranda 60, 61
Japanese aralia 14

L
Laurel, Australian 64
  Indian 11
Loquat, Chinese 66

M
Mexican breadfruit plant 50
Monstera 50, 51
Moss, club 66
Myrtle, common 16, 17

O
Oak, silk 57, 64, 65

P
Palms 38–46
Palm, canary date 44, 45
  Chinese fan 46
  coconut 42
  date 43, 44
  desert fan 46
  fishtail 41
  lady 65
  miniature 45
  oil 43
  parlor 38, 39
  petticoat 46
  pigmy 45
  ponytail 52
  sugar 43
  thread 46
  yellow 40
Paper-rush, Egyptian 4
Philodendron 28–31, 50
  'Green emerald' 30
  heart-leaf 28, 31
  'Red emerald' 30
  split-leaf 28, 31
Piggyback plant 65
Pine, Norfolk Island 32, 33
  screw 47

R
Rubber plant 6, 7

S
Sago plant 48
Spanish bayonet 62
Starleaf 57
Swiss cheese plant 28, 50

T
Trevesia 14, 15

U
Umbrella plant 4, 5
  dwarf 4
Umbrella tree, Queensland 57, 58

V
Vine, chestnut 66, 67
Violet, African 34

Y
Yucca 62, 63
  spineless 57, 62, 63

ACKNOWLEDGMENTS

Publisher	**Bruce Marshall**	Contributors	**Donald Binney** **Barbara Segal**
Creative Director	**John Bigg**	Text Editing	**Jinny Johnson**
Editor	**Anne Kilborn**	Picture Editor	**Zilda Tandy**
Managing Editor	**Ruth Binney**	Production Coordination	**Barry Baker** **Janice Storr**
Art Editor	**Pauline Faulks**		

Torstar Books Inc.
41 Madison Avenue
Suite 2900
New York, NY 10010

Marshall Editions, an editorial group that specializes in the design and publication of practical and scientific subjects for the general reader, prepared this book in collaboration with ICA-förlaget AB, Sweden. Marshall has written and illustrated standard works on gardening, cookery, needlecraft, photography, biology and technology which are recommended for schools and libraries, as well as for popular reference.

Series Consultant **Maggie Oster** is advisor to *The Complete Gardening Guide* and has written extensively on the subjects of plants and gardens. She was a major contributor to the *Time-Life Encyclopedia of Gardening* and from 1982–83 was producer and presenter of the monthly television show "Maggie's Garden" on WLKY-TV.

Photographs
Cover photograph Spike Powell
Photograph pp. 2–3 Spike Powell
All other photography
courtesy ICA-förlaget AB

Artwork
pp. 4, 13, 16, 21, 31, 36, 51, 54 Norman Bancroft-Hunt
pp. 64–69 Karen Daws/John Craddock ACA
Endpapers Hayward and Martin

Plants and containers
Plants: cover, pp. 2–3 Longmans Ltd,
container: cover Casa Catalan